THE ILLUMINATED MIND

THE ILLUMINATED MIND

A Step-by-Step Guide to Spiritual Discovery

by

June d'Estelle, Ph.D.

Alohem Publishing Company
Cotati, California

ISBN 0–941407–00–4

Illustrations: Nalani Waikiki

Alohem Publishing Company
Cotati, California 1987

CONTENTS

ACKNOWLEDGEMENTS   vii
PREFACE   ix
INTRODUCTION   1

SECTION I — GETTING STARTED

CHAPTER 1.   AN OVERVIEW OF THE
              COURSE   9
CHAPTER 2.   GLIMPSING TECHNIQUES
              AND PROCEDURES:
              WHAT LIES AHEAD   12
CHAPTER 3.   KEY TO THE INNER REALMS   21
CHAPTER 4.   PREPATTERNING SLEEP   31

SECTION II — TAKING CHARGE

CHAPTER 5.   THE POWER OF THOUGHT   37
CHAPTER 6.   MODEL THE CHILD AND
              YOU FORM THE ADULT   46
CHAPTER 7.   CREATING YOUR INNER WORKSHOP   53
CHAPTER 8.   INNER LEARNING   57
CHAPTER 9.   RESOLVING PROBLEMS   64
CHAPTER 10.   PROGRAMMING   72
CHAPTER 11.   REPROGRAMMING HABITS   79
CHAPTER 12.   RELEASING ADDICTIONS   90
CHAPTER 13.   SURRENDER   112

SECTION III — SPREADING THE LIGHT

CHAPTER 14.   WHITE LIGHT   125
CHAPTER 15.   MEETING YOUR
              SPIRITUAL GUIDES   139
CHAPTER 16.   THE INNER WORLD OF
              GEMS AND FLOWERS,
              MINERALS AND PLANTS   151
CHAPTER 17.   THE INNER WORLD OF
              ANIMALS   157
CHAPTER 18.   TELEPATHY   167
CHAPTER 19.   INNER ANATOMY   177
CHAPTER 20.   REMOTE HEALING   183
CHAPTER 21.   CONCLUSION BUT JUST BEGINNING   197

ACKNOWLEDGEMENTS

This book is dedicated to my parents
Virginia and Chester Estill

and to all those who have loved and helped me. My deepest appreciation:

To Dr. Peter Navarro
To Della Heide
To Sandra Giesen
To Janice Edwards
To my children, Carole, Jeffrey,
Lauren and Alan

To my niece, Nalani Waikiki, for her gifted art work and her help on all dimensions.

In a special category by himself, my heartfelt gratitude to Dr. Scott Rogers, whose talented assistance and support made this book manifest. The inspiration of our meditations together sustained the spiritual guidance underlying these pages.

. . . rise to the heights which are your birthright . . .

PREFACE

"Be ye transformed by the renewing of your mind."

(Romans 12:2)

During the several years I have taught "Seminars in the Illuminated Mind", I have been privileged to witness the evolution and unfolding of the material presented in this book. The experiences in my own life and the growth of my students have been truly remarkable.

In the midst of daily living, it is easy to take for granted events and benefactions which in retrospect appear extraordinary and profound. I will not burden the reader with a recital of spectacular phenomena; that is not the purpose of this writing.

Rather I would emphasize that everything proposed in this text has been verified repeatedly in the experience of students, colleagues and myself. It will be proven to you as well if you apply yourself to the exercises given and are open to the results.

Because of the incredible wealth of current research in psychology, parapsychology, biology and related fields, I have interwoven my work with explanations gleaned from these areas of scientific inquiry. However, I am well aware that much of what I have found true through teaching and personal experience is not yet scientifically proven, for much of it does not lend itself readily to the methodologies of scientific investigation.

ix

Nor have I tried to provide extensive or detailed interpretation and references for the research material mentioned in this book. The interested reader will find numerous books and publications which can do far greater justice to the rigors of scientific investigation than I can cover within the context of this book.

I encourage each reader to discover the relevance and benefit of the methods, techniques and philosophy introduced in this manual. In the final analysis, it does not matter what has been proven or disproven for others.

What matters is your own discovery of the way in which the tools can work for you, and how they may be applied in your life, for one of the greatest rewards of the whole learning experience is finding one's own path.

INTRODUCTION

The book you hold in your hand is worth a King's ransom. Your ancestors would have given all they possessed to have read its pages. For within its covers is revealed knowledge for which they would have depleted their fortunes and sacrificed their lives to obtain.

This book is not just another manuscript describing the teachings of the past, nor the incoming wonders of the New Age. This is an actual manual for enlightenment, a handbook which will conduct you step-by-step through an accelerated course toward illumination.

The most closely guarded secrets of the past are here presented to you in a wholly modern, methodical series of exercises which will catapult you safely from the indecisiveness of the present into the awakened consciousness of the future. All you need to do is read the book and perform the exercises, which themselves are easy, pleasant and exciting.

Your ancestors would have treasured the teachings you will be discovering, but would have found the exercises disconcerting, for they would have been too potent for the Earth's vibrational field of their time. Only now, for our generation, is this book possible.

Why is this true? Why are we so privileged? Why are we given this unprecedented opportunity?

We are living in a time of unparalleled magic and splendor. A new consciousness is awakening upon the earth, surging through the spirit and heart of mankind like a vast majestic wave. This stupendous tide is opening doors which

have long been sealed, drawing veils from the most sacred of
mysteries. Because we are living at this precise chronological
moment, as this new consciousness is beginning to emerge,
we have opportunities unprecedented within the memory of
man. We have the power and option to take control of our
own destinies.

We are participating in the most momentous event in the
history of mankind. Earth, with humanity enfolded, is
moving ceremoniously into a higher vibratory field, into an
exalted state of consciousness far surpassing anything which
our limited intelligence can begin to comprehend. We are
entering the time of fulfillment of prophecy, a time long
foretold and fervently desired. A new race is being born, a
new world is in the making.

In a stately promenade of the galaxies, our solar system,
with Earth as the pivotal point, is beginning the final
movements of a royal dance of the ages. Messengers of Light
have gathered from the ends of the universe to join the finale
of this grand pageant, which will culminate in the
transformation of Earth and humanity from one state of
being into another.

All of us now living upon the earth have key roles to play
in this triumphant conclusion. Each of us has an individual
mission to perform, and the time in which to accomplish this
mission is brief. The most rewarding task you can undertake
is the search for and fulfillment of your own contribution to
destiny.

When you commit yourself to this goal, your life will
change dramatically. No longer will you need to vacillate
and equivocate, for a Higher Intelligence will impel you
firmly and truly in the right direction. All of the guidance
and assistance you require will be provided.

In dedicating yourself to your life's main purpose, you will
be commencing the most wondrous of all missions, the
search to discover and uncover the full glory of your own
higher nature.

The Journey

The route is systematic and true. It has been known throughout the ages, but heretofore has been shrouded in mystery. Now, at this golden moment in time, this mystical way can be revealed freely and openly. Esoteric knowledge once confined to a few towering saints or deeply imbedded in ancient teachings, is for the first time in recorded history readily available for all who seek.

Through countless centuries, the hidden techniques of personal transformation have been guarded and protected, painstakingly revealed to only a few ardent seekers who were totally committed to a demanding regime of rigorous testing, initiations and gruelling study. Such precautions were essential and prudent, for the powers unleashed by these techniques are immensely potent, and must be skillfully integrated into a seeker's personality. When properly channeled and harmonized, however, these forces bring fulfillment and infinite joy.

We are now entering a new age, in which most of humanity is ready to embrace the knowledge of the deep mysteries, and to transform not only individual lives, but Earth itself into a wondrous heritage of enlightenment.

You are about to join this great adventure. This book will take you upon a very special journey, perhaps the most rewarding venture of your life. You will be guided through a simple, proven system of inner unfoldment, which will lead you swiftly and safely along the pathway to higher awareness. No previous experience in metaphysical techniques is necessary; no belief or faith is required, beyond an openness to explore and see for yourself. You will find the vistas extraordinary.

A Unique Period

This unique interlude in the evolutionary history of mankind is the most propitious of all times to undertake this project, for you will be receiving special assistance from higher powers. Cosmic energies now flooding the earth have never before been encountered by the human race. These are energies which lead to upliftment or upheaval, for energy can be used for either positive or negative purposes. The world as we know it is ending. We are witnessing the beginning of a new world whose promise we can scarcely imagine. All around us, vast disruptions are altering the very structure of our civilization. These changes are reflected within our own natures, as we discard the selves we formerly were and become fresh, new, unfamiliar beings. Whether we will it or not, transformation is taking place. As the vibratory rate of the earth increases, we must raise our own vibrations in order to survive.

Path of the Initiate

Each of us faces a crucial decision. You may elect to drift with the masses of humanity, tossed haphazardly by the tides and winds of change. If you so choose, you will enter the new age through chaos and turbulance, immersed in the destruction of the old age as Earth is purged in preparation for the birth of the new. Or you may elect to chart your own course, bypassing the turmoil, and effortlessly, exultantly, ride the crest of this mighty wave into the Golden Age.

When you decide to take your destiny into your own hands, you create a major turning point in your life, for you will be venturing upon a noble, sharply ascending path. This path is known traditionally as the Path of the Initiate.

In the past, aspirants were required to pledge their entire lives to the pursuit of enlightenment. Your search will still require commitment and effort, but its course will be encapsulated. Within a fraction of the time formerly required, you may attain the goal which has been the object of man's highest and most reverent quest throughout the centuries.

Signs of the New Age

For time itself is changing, increasing its tempo, speeding up. Accelerated learning has become an accepted phenomenon of our generation. We now experience in months or weeks what we formerly experienced in years. These are signs of the New Age, as is the great outpouring of knowledge which is threatening to engulf us.

We are evolving at such rapid rates in all directions that we have to go beyond the scope of our conscious, rational minds in order to understand ourselves, to cope with our burgeoning lives. The purpose of this book is to show you how to accomplish this. Through its modern adaptations of age-old techniques, you will rise to the mastery of your life.

Such self-mastery demands that you uplift and harmonize all aspects of yourself as you reach for perfection and wholeness. In refining and developing your higher nature, you will simultaneously focus your growing powers upon the solution of worldly concerns. The growth you attain on the inner dimensions will be reflected in the transformation of your outer world.

Have no fears that you may be embarking upon an isolated, lonely journey. You are instead joining a rapidly swelling throng, for men and women everywhere are discovering these old-new techniques and applying them to everyday issues and to their highest visions. Since awareness exists in the totality of our beings, they are resolving their most perplexing problems and improving the material conditions of their lives, but their greatest reward is a new profound understanding of who they really are.

As you read this book you will learn to use these same processes, and through your own experiences, the only avenue which really carries total conviction, you will prove to yourself that these techniques are reliable and effective, that beyond any question or doubt, they truly work.

The methods you will be exploring are in keeping with the

prevailing acceleration and sense of urgency. The techniques are uncomplicated and can be easily understood by anyone. They condense into hours, processes for inner growth which in the past required many years of intensive study. You will be learning to contact an inner part of yourself which is already fully developed, complete with infinite wisdom and limitless potential. You do not have to evolve to higher consciousness — you are already there. You are commencing a journey of discovery, an engrossing search through the major realms of your consciousness. You will be clearing, integrating and acknowledging these realms as you recognize and attune to the divinity within.

The path of self-acceptance and realization is wondrous and great, absorbing and beautiful, the finest adventure you can hope to undertake. The rewards are magnificent, for in the end, you come face to face with your own Sacred Being, and realize you have served it all along.

SECTION I
GETTING STARTED

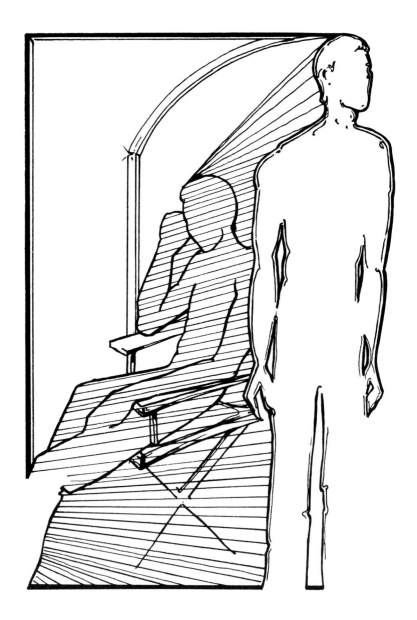

. . . the realization that all things are possible comes
through the process of changing the self . . .

CHAPTER 1
WHAT WILL YOU BE
LEARNING?

W hat are these procedures? What is the program? The underlying theme of all you will be doing is learning to harness and direct the immense and awesome creative power of your thoughts, and to awaken the divinity within you.

As you follow the instructions you will be guided through a series of intriguing experiences which will bring into manifestation your real self, the glorious essence which slumbers within you. That bright new self is stirring, seeking to emerge.

Because of the powerful energies of this time, you will progress at an incredible pace. The systematic procedures you will be learning are the easiest way we know to align with these mighty forces of change and to move swiftly and gracefully into higher realms of consciousness.

This is not a book to be read casually and set aside. It is instead a book you will refer to, will read again and again. As you progress through its pages you will learn to know yourself in a different way, uncovering new dimensions of yourself and revealing talents and abilities you never knew existed.

Here is an outline of the program you will be following, beginning with the art of relaxation, which will serve as a foundation for all subsequent exercises. The other steps will be developed as we go through the book.

We will focus upon these major areas:

1. Relaxing, for the art of mental and physical relaxation is essential to inner development.
2. Altering your states of consciousness voluntarily through establishing control of your sleeping habits.
3. Stimulating dormant areas of your mind: expanding your intellect, enhancing your memory, increasing your learning abilities.
4. Exploring techniques for changing habits easily and resolving problems through the inner resources of your mind.
5. Redesigning your affairs, including those of the material world.
6. Mastering new skills, excelling in physical activities and sports, perfecting your talents.
7. Experiencing greater harmony in your relationships, improving your health, simplifying tasks.
8. Awakening your intuition, which will establish clear channels to the sources of inspiration and creativity in any area you choose (designing, composing, writing, or inventing).
9. Learning telepathic and mental communication, then applying these skills for self-improvement as well as for assisting others.
10. Acquiring a deeper communication with nature through perceiving the structure and functions of minerals, plants and animals from an inner viewpoint.
11. Developing the art of intuitive assessment and spiritual healing.
12. Meeting your spiritual guides. The goal toward which you will be constantly moving, attunement to the divinity within and to an all-loving, nurturing Presence, is advanced immeasurably through meeting these beautiful ethereal beings who guard and inspire you.

The focus of the entire process is the unveiling of the skills and potentials of your emerging self, while unfolding brilliant new facets of Being.

Based on principles of Truth, all the exercises progress in total safety. While these principles have formed an integral part of ancient esoteric teaching, they emerge here in a new modern setting, geared to the tempo of today and available for all to use.

The design of the program is for gradual, persistent and consistent growth and development of your inner self. Thus the book serves also as a manual for resolving the issues of daily living as you create harmonious environs for this unfoldment.

When you have finished the book and practiced the exercises, you will have in your possession valuable aids which will enable you to assume command of yourself, to consciously govern and direct your life. However, your highest reward will be the discovery of the answer to the question, "Who am I?".

Whatever your starting point, as a beginner or as a veteran of consciousness studies, this book will help you to expand and grow. You will progress at your own pace, for each person's path is uniquely his own.

CHAPTER 2
GLIMPSING TECHNIQUES
AND PROCEDURES

How is this undertaking to be accomplished? How can you, in a brief time, reach the goal of Self-discovery which has been the ultimate dream of the world's greatest thinkers and most dedicated souls? We remind you again that all of this is possible because of the wonderful good fortune we share in being born at this specific period in the evolution of the human race. We are living in an unparalleled time, a time of wonder and enchantment, a magical time when it is becoming more and more apparent that all things are possible.

You will be using methods which are extremely potent, utilizing tools which are already in your possession. You use a fraction of the capacity of these gifts daily, with little conception of their true potential. Now you will learn to become adept in the use of these tools to uncover within yourself hidden layers of consciousness wherein untold powers reside.

You will build upon a framework which has proven effective for others, but will develop your own pattern and achieve your own individualized results.

Layers of Consciousness

This rapid growth is possible because of the remarkable complexity of your mind. You are a composite being, made up of multiple layers of consciousness, with capabilities and resources of which most of us are unaware. You are wondrously and awesomely made. Beyond the everyday self lie other selves, gifted with wisdom and knowledge, individualistic and yet intrinsically part of you.

Three Aspects of Man

What are these mysterious other selves? How do they function? Your consciousness is actually divided into three distinct and separate states of being. In all cultures and lands this premise runs as a consistent theme through myths, legends, religious and esoteric teachings.

Many descriptive names have been given to these three aspects, all reflecting the concept of a lower, a middle, and a higher realm of being. For example, the Polynesians, whose culture encircled the globe, described these divisions aptly, as:

1. The Low Self, or "Unihipili";
2. The Middle Self, or "Uhane";
3. The High Self, or "Aumakua".

In modern psychology, Carl Jung depicted this same trinity as:

1. The subconscious mind;
2. The conscious mind;
3. The superconscious mind.

Because your understanding of these divisions is crucial, we will explore them briefly.

The Low Self or Subconscious Mind

Your Lower Self, or subconscious mind, is that mysterious part of your being in which reside your emotions, memories and habits. This intrinsic part of yourself is under the jurisdiction of a great intelligence, which orders and maintains the incredible complexity of your bodily processes. This intelligence is governed by instinct rather than logic; it manifests psychic awareness, attuning you to nature and to your earthly heritage.

Your Low Self is a willing servant, receptive to the commands of the Middle and High Selves, and is faithful in carrying out their directives.

You live mostly in the domain of the Low Self during childhood, gradually maturing through adolescence as you develop and incorporate the more extended capacities of your Middle Self.

The Middle Self or Conscious Mind

Like most of us, you undoubtedly focus your awareness primarily in your conscious mind, or Middle Self. This is the domain of your intellect . . . of rational, logical thinking; the domain of time, of space, of your five senses. Through these avenues you experience and direct your outer world. To the average person, this is the only reality, the "real world".

The High Self or Superconscious Mind

Beyond the range of the Low and Middle Selves is another part of your being which few of us recognize. This is the High Self, or superconscious mind.

The High Self is the divinity within you . . . the soul, the spirit, the Being of Light which spiritual teachers regard as your true Self.

The High Self is all-knowing, all-loving, radiant and beautiful. Through it you express inspiration, creativity, and such higher emotions as compassion, gentleness, benevolence and understanding. Through the High Self you express Love, and eventually Enlightenment.

The Higher Self and the Lesser Self

The High or Higher Self is the over-all guiding intelligence which oversees your destiny, which knows your purpose for living against the backdrop of eternity. Because together the Low and Middle Selves, the subconscious and conscious minds, manifest the intelligence and form which enable you to survive and function upon the earth, we speak of them together as the Lesser Self. Ideally your Lesser Self will rise up and become one with your Higher Self, unifying the totality of your being so that you function thereafter from that exalted level.

Your Lower and Middle Selves must first be in harmony and balance before you can attune to the High Self. This imperative is the underlying purpose behind several of the exercises you will be doing. You will learn to establish direct communication between your conscious and subconscious minds, which will enable you to recognize and remove those conditions which impede your progress. You will be taught how to purify your body, stabilize your emotions, etc.

You will be exploring these three realms of consciousness, discovering their beauty and immense possibilities, then expanding, harmonizing, and finally uniting these different levels of awareness into a single sense of self. You are actually laying the foundation for enlightenment.

The Worlds of Your Inner Self and Outer Self

The role of our conscious minds is to take capable charge of the affairs of our daily lives, in which most of us are usually engrossed. Because of this outward focus, we refer to the conscious mind and its involvements as the "outer self".

The subconscious and superconscious minds together form the world of the inner self, which normally is reached in moments of repose or relaxation. When your thoughts turn inward in meditation or contemplation or when you are absorbed in music or flights of fancy, you are in the realm of the inner self.

As you learn to enter this inner world voluntarily by means of the exercises in this book, you will automatically inherit the unique benefits indwelling this realm. To glimpse briefly some of those benefits:

1. You will begin to develop five inner senses corresponding to the five outer senses, which will enable you to experience your new world. A range of new sensations will evolve.
2. You will develop increasing powers of concentration, keener perception, a more positive state of mind.
3. With developing intuition, you will be enabled to make decisions easily and accurately, will be able to cause things to happen at will. Telepathy and thought transference will become common and useful modes of expression.
4. This inner world is the level of inspiration and creativity; your entire life will be uplifted through reaching this realm.

Suggestions for Success

When you are ready to begin the actual exercises, these suggestions will help to insure your success:

1. Find a private place in which to study and practice the exercises. It is important that you be undisturbed while in deep levels of consciousness.
2. Take a few moments to prepare yourself before beginning each session. Clear your mind of distracting thoughts and concerns, free yourself from the affairs of the outer world.
3. Let your attitude be receptive and expectant, for feelings of doubt will create an atmosphere which will prevent the manifestations you are seeking. Your own experiences

will soon provide the most convincing proof of the validity of the processes.

4. One important point must be emphasized: you may find it fascinating to read about the concepts and the procedures which demonstrate them. However, you will obtain optimum results only by going through the training processes and actually *doing* the exercises, not by intellectual understanding alone. You must have practical conditioning in order to acquire these new abilities and establish clear communication with your inner self.

5. Follow the exercises in the exact order in which they are presented. They are placed in a special sequence which is designed to build systematically a firm foundation for the work which will follow. Each technique evolves from those which have preceded it. You will notice an increase in energy, a quickening of vibration as you move through the processes step by step.

Design of Exercises

The first exercise will teach you to relax completely at will. From that essential beginning you will be led through various exercises into progressively deeper and deeper levels of awareness. For example, you may appreciate the convenience of learning to control your sleeping habits, but you are actually acquiring the ability to voluntarily select and control your states of consciousness.

In one chapter you will mentally create a special workshop in which to do your self-transformational work. Even though it apparently exists only in your imagination, this will become a very real place. It can actually be seen by clairvoyants who are trained to see mental images or thought-forms.

In this mental workshop you will discover the powers of the Lesser Self, will learn to direct and work with those powers, and to use them to embellish your life.

You will acquire special techniques for resolving problems intuitively, and will develop your creativity along with your intuition.

Then from a point of greater understanding of the powers you may command, you will consciously relinquish control of your life to higher unseen superconscious guidance. Included will be telepathic communication and projection, and you will meet and establish a harmonious rapport with your spiritual guides.

This will prepare you for the culminating exercises in intuitive assessment and healing, which utilize all the abilities you have developed.

As you practice the final procedures, you will be consolidating the knowledge and skills you have attained. They will become second-nature — deeply rooted and comfortably taken for granted.

Because the experiences have been drawn from many disciplines and ancient teachings, they are effective, proven and dependable. Some of them may be much more meaningful to you at one time than at another. Later you may reread the book and find the solution to a current problem in an exercise you may have previously dismissed as unimportant.

The techniques you will be learning are the outgrowth of a series of successful seminars in personal and spiritual development, courses which have been presented to thousands of people over the past several years.

The ideal situation, of course, would be to study these exercises under the personal direction of an inspired teacher, with the greatly enhanced energy of a supportive group. The progress of those who experience such training is truly spectacular. However, since the number of those who have the opportunity to attend these seminars personally is limited, an excellent and very satisfactory alternative is to study the identical course as it is presented in this book.

You will be going through the same processes, doing the

same exercises as the participants in the training seminars. The work in the seminars is necessarily condensed and concentrated into a brief period of time, which provides particular advantages. On the other hand, you will have the special opportunity to work at your own speed and in your own time.

So be prepared for a wonderfully exciting and productive experience! Enjoy yourself!

relax

CHAPTER 3
RELAXATION — KEY
TO THE INNER REALMS

I t is time to take the first step in communicating with your inner self — you are ready to learn the art of relaxation. This skill is of primary importance, for in order to reach deeper levels of consciousness, you must be able to relax your body and mind completely by simply desiring to do so.

In this chapter you will learn techniques which enable you to reach complete physical relaxation within moments, just by taking one deep breath and telling yourself to relax.

Mental relaxation involves a more subtle approach than does physical relaxation. Your mind is normally active: busy with thoughts, tensing muscles, arousing emotions or causing distraction by reviewing the issues and problems of your life. Nevertheless, gently and pleasantly, you will learn to quiet and focus your thoughts. You will be communicating directly with your inner mind in its own language, through visualization and imagination.

Mental relaxation can be induced in part by visualizing restful, passive scenes, then projecting yourself into the scenes through your imagination. By vivid use of your inner senses, you will soon feel as if you are actually there. This technique not only produces mental relaxation, it also serves as an excellent stimulus for further awakening and developing these inner senses.

Importance of Relaxation

Relaxation is a valuable skill to learn for its own sake. Many of us have hidden areas of tension of which we remain unaware. If this tension is released through massage, saunas, or other physical methods, we usually experience a wonderful sensation of peace and well-being. Now you will be able to recapture this feeling of contentment and well-being at will, whenever and wherever you desire.

As you practice this system of relaxation, you will also be learning an accelerated method for reaching a deep meditative level quickly, within seconds. Most meditators can attain this desired peaceful state only through special processes which involve a certain amount of time, and which require considerable study and effort to learn. As you move through this book, you will be able to descend to far deeper levels of consciousness than you have previously entered, and to return from these depths instantly.

Usually, those who meditate expect to spend a little time after deep meditation in centering and returning fully to the outer world. You will not need this refocusing interlude, for you will be balanced, centered, and normally alert immediately upon concluding your exercise.

If you have never meditated before, you will discover that this level of awareness is highly rewarding, for it is energizing and rejuvenating. Even a brief period of meditation will leave you feeling composed, serene, and wonderfully refreshed. Traditional meditation is usually passive and receptive; you will be supplementing this method with a new form of active, dynamic meditation. At first you will use a preprogrammed formula technique, but very shortly you will drop into a deeper state instantly by simply taking a deep breath and telling yourself to relax.

Relaxation is a prerequisite for effective functioning in many areas of life, such as in sports. Those who excel physically and mentally have learned to exert tension, then release it and relax completely. Many physical maladies can be traced to the inability to release excessive tension once the need for that tension is past.

In almost all disciplines working with the subconscious mind and using techniques enabling one to reach these deep levels of relaxation, special attention is given to two important factors: posture and breathing. Both strongly influence the effectiveness of meditation and relaxation. Before we do the relaxation exercise itself we will take a few moments to review the techniques of posture and breathing used in all the exercises. In spite of their importance, the forms we will be employing are simple and logical.

Posture

Sit in a comfortable position, with your back straight, your head erect, balanced and unstrained over your spine. Uncross your arms and legs and place your feet flat upon the floor. Rest your arms upon your lap or upon the arms of a chair. You may sit in the lotus or modified lotus positions if they are comfortable for you.

Your goal is to have your body centered and balanced, so that you may enter deep states of relaxation without discomfort or strain. An erect spine also permits subtle body energies to flow freely without interference or blockage. In such a secure position you can become engrossed in your inward exercises and meditations, well insulated from bodily distractions.

Some people like to meditate lying down, which normally is an excellent way to encourage relaxation. However, you are developing through the studies in this book, the ability to reach this stage of consciousness and relaxation at any time, in any position. We have discovered that those who learn these techniques while in a prone position must henceforth lie down whenever they wish to apply them. If you learn these techniques while sitting up, however, you will be able to use them anytime, whether sitting, lying down, walking, driving your car, or participating in other activities.

Breathing

Breathing is another very important consideration in relaxation and meditation. If you have paid little attention to your breath, you probably have developed the habit of shallow breathing, and seldom fill your lungs completely. A much more healthful pattern of deeper breathing will become established as you practice the following exercises.

With each exercise you will begin with deep breaths, inhaling as if your entire body were hollow, and imagining that you are filling it with air clear down to your toes. With each exhalation, you will release all of the entrapped air, leaving you with a renewed feeling of calmness and well-being.

You will be delighted with the increased vitality and sense of cleanliness which tingles throughout your body as you replace stale air with fresh. You are charging all of your cells with a special vital energy (sometimes called prana) which enters your lungs with your breath.

Now you are ready to do your first exercise, the basic relaxation process which is fundamental to all of the techniques which will follow. We will progress at an easy pace, with pauses after each instruction.

Relaxation Exercise

1. Select a quiet, private place where you will be undisturbed.
2. Sit in a comfortable position, and close your eyes.
3. Now take a deep breath and hold it . . . then let it out with a sigh.
4. Take another deep breath, and hold it . . . then let it out with a sigh.
5. Take another deep breath, and hold it . . . then let it out at your own time and pace.
6. You are now at a deeper, healthier level of mind.

7. You will now count backward slowly from ten to one. Each descending number will take you to a deeper and still deeper level of mind.
   10....9....8....7....6....5....4....3....2....1
   You have reached a deeper, healthier level of mind.

8. Now imagine a soft, warm shower of water pouring down over your body, carrying with it all tension and pressure. Concentrate your attention upon your scalp, and as the tightness and pressure dissolve and melt away, let your scalp relax completely. Move your attention slowly downward, and focus upon your forehead. Feel all of the tension drain away with the smooth, warm shower. The shower creates a tingling, vibrating sensation as it flows over your face.

9. With the soothing water caressing your face, relax your cheeks . . . relax your ears . . . relax your jaw . . . relax your tongue. . .

10. Relax your eyes . . . relax your eyelids . . . your eyebrows . . . relax all of the muscles and tissues around your eyes, including the eyeballs themselves. . .

11. This warm wave of relaxation flows slowly down your neck, down your throat, dissolving all tension, leaving behind a tingling, vibrating sensation. . .

12. Relax your shoulders . . . release all tightness, all pressure . . . the tingling, vibrating sensation is flowing down your arms and your hands, as you relax your arms and your hands. . .

13. Now let the warm wave flow down your back, drawing with it all tightness, all tension. . .

14. Relax your chest . . . feel the tingling, vibrating sensation flowing down your chest, as you release all tension all pressure . . . feel it pouring down your abdomen, as you completely relax. . .

15. Relax your pelvis and your buttocks, releasing all tension, all pressure. . .

16. Relax all of your internal organs . . . every gland, every

organ, every cell of your body is functioning in a perfectly rhythmic and healthy manner as you release all excess tension, all pressure. . .

17. Imagine soft, caressing water pouring delightfully over your body as you relax your thighs . . . relax your knees . . . relax your calves . . . relax your feet. . .

18. Your entire body is completely and totally relaxed. The flowing, soothing water, the tingling, vibrating sensation, is enveloping your whole body as you completely relax. You are floating on a warm, buoyant sea, safe and secure. . .

19. Release your limbs . . . let them float upon the water . . . your arms and legs feel as if they do not belong to you . . . your whole body is released and free . . . you are comfortable . . . you are warm . . . you are supported . . . you are completely and totally relaxed.

20. You will reach this same state of complete relaxation every time you take a deep breath and tell yourself to relax. Whenever you take a deep breath and tell yourself to relax, your body and mind will relax completely, as they are relaxed now.

* * * * * * * * * * * * * * * * * * * *

While you are practicing this method of guided relaxation, you may find it helpful to make a tape recording of the exercise. Then let the recording guide you through the steps instead of directing yourself mentally. Omit the step numbers on the tape. You will probably relax more readily and thoroughly when your mind is permitted to be completely receptive, freed from the responsibility of directing.

Repeat this exercise, practice it frequently for a brief time. It is pleasant, rewarding, and the repetition will soon train your inner mind to respond instantly to the command to relax your body.

The next technique, the process for attaining mental relaxation, is especially enjoyable, for you will be directing your attention to a quiet, restful scene.

Mental Relaxation Exercise

1. Begin by relaxing your body, as you did in the preceding exercise.
2. Now imagine yourself in a beautiful, peaceful place, an actual place you remember or a fantasy scene you create in your imagination. Use all of your inner senses to experience it fully, in minute detail. Sense the scene so vividly that you feel as if you are actually there. Your role is to be a passive participant rather than an active one.
3. For example: imagine yourself lying on the beach on a sunny summer day. Sense the warm sand beneath your body, the welcome heat of the sun beating down upon you. Feel the softness of the air, a gentle, caressing breeze. Listen to the waves . . . the sound of the surf against the shore. Hear the cries of the seagulls, the sweet trills of distant songbirds. . .
4. Lick your lips . . . taste the salt. Now inhale deeply . . . smell the salt air . . . the fragrance of flowers.
5. Take your time, create a clear impression. Imagine that you are really there.

* *

With this exercise you are learning to focus your attention and to relax your mind, but other skills are being developed as well. You are awakening your imagination and expanding the range of your inner senses of touch, taste, sight, hearing and smell. As you practice, you will increase the vividness of the impression so that you will almost believe you are actually there.

This will become a very real place, a retreat for you. Whenever you find yourself in a harried, distracted emotional condition, pause for a few moments, relax your body, then project yourself to your peaceful place. You will return refreshed, renewed, calm, and at peace.

This state of inner quietude is your meditative level, a

level of being ideally conducive to meditation and introspection.

When you establish contact with the inner self, it is just as important to come out of a deep meditative state quickly, at will, as it is to enter that state rapidly. Soon you will be using this level of consciousness constantly in your daily affairs. You will become adept at dropping instantly into the inner level, directing your attention to the goals you wish to accomplish, then returning immediately to your normal outer state of being. Your skill in returning rapidly will develop in step with your increasing ability to enter deeper levels, for you will practice the coming-out technique every time you do the physical-mental relaxation exercise.

Coming-Out Exercise

When you are ready to come out of a meditative state, repeat the following instructions to your inner mind:

1. "I will now count from one to five. When I open my eyes, I will be wide awake, feeling fine and in perfect health; feeling happy, alert, energetic; feeling centered and balanced, in tune with life."
2. Count slowly: "1 ... 2 ... 3"
3. At the count of 3, remind yourself again: "I am counting to five. When I reach the count of 5, I will open my eyes, be wide awake, feeling fine and in perfect health; feeling happy, alert, energetic; feeling centered and balanced, in tune with life ... 4 ... 5"
4. Open your eyes. You will be wide awake, alert, centered and grounded.

* * * * * * * * * * * * * * * * * *

Practice the methods of physical and mental relaxation and the coming-out technique together, regularly. Within a short time, you will be able to reach a deep state of relaxation easily and confidently. You are ready then to shorten the procedure. The following exercise is to be done only after you have worked for a period of time with the more comprehensive preceding techniques.

Exercise: Reaching your Meditative Level, Accelerated Method

1. Close your eyes . . . take a deep breath . . . now instruct your inner mind:
2. "Relax . . . each exhalation will drain all excess tension from my body. My mind is tranquil and clear."
3. Almost immediately, you will be in a restful, peaceful state of relaxation. In a particularly stressful situation, repeat the deep breathing two or three times. You may also enhance your relaxation by counting backward slowly from ten to one.
4. Attune to your peaceful place; experience its tranquility.
5. You have reached your meditative level, ready to meditate or proceed with your inner exercises.
6. When you have finished your meditation, you may come out just as rapidly. Take a deep breath, open your eyes, and tell yourself, "I am wide awake, feeling fine and in perfect health, feeling perfectly centered and grounded." As you open your eyes, you will find yourself alert and clear, back in your normal world.

* * * * * * * * * * * * * * * * * * * *

By the time you have finished reading the book and doing the exercises, you will probably find that you no longer need to do any special exercise in order to become completely relaxed. You will simply take a deep breath, tell yourself to relax, and as you exhale, all of your excessive tension, physical and mental, will disappear. You can then be in your meditative level with your eyes open as easily as you can with them closed.

Later, you will drop down into deeper levels merely by

desiring to do so, and will readjust automatically to the outer world when the need for deepening is over.

Eventually, with repeated practice, you will enter and return from these deeper levels habitually, without conscious direction, whenever the need arises.

At this point, you have retrained your mind to cope more efficiently with the demands of living. Your responses in this regard will be just as spontaneous as those automatic reflexes which enable you to maneuver your car efficiently through rapidly changing traffic. All that is required is continuing practice in every possible situation, and the unwavering desire to grow.

CHAPTER 4
PREPATTERNING SLEEP

N ow that you have learned to relax at will and to
attain deeper levels of consciousness, you can
begin communicating directly with your inner self.
Because this contact bypasses the rational mind, your inner
self will be cooperative and responsive.

You will establish this communication gradually through
the use of simple, non-threatening exercises. The first of
these will teach you to control your sleeping patterns. Since
your inner mind already regulates your sleeping habits, it
will readily accept your suggestions to alter these patterns.

From this easy, secure beginning, you will establish a deep
rapport between your conscious mind and your inner self,
enabling the two to cooperate harmoniously in the more
complex techniques to come.

You will learn the formula for sleep control very quickly,
sometimes with dramatic results. In numerous classes,
students with lifelong histories of insomnia have found deep,
restful sleep after practicing this technique only a few times,
with no need for medications or soporifics. Others gratefully
develop the ability to waken refreshed and alert after a long
history of grumpy, groggy mornings.

As you work with the techniques over a period of time,
your intentions become firmly impressed in your inner mind.
Soon the formulas will no longer be necessary, and can be
replaced with simple suggestions to trigger the desired response.

With minimal practice you can learn to:
— Induce sleep swiftly, and eliminate insomnia;
— Awaken at any predesignated time, without an alarm;

— Stay awake as long as you wish to accomplish projects;
— Take catnaps which refresh you as fully as an entire night's sleep.

The meditative level you are using to alter your sleep habits is rejuvenating and rebuilding. You may find that as you spend more time in this level during your waking hours, you will naturally require fewer hours of sleep at night. Substantial changes in your overall schedule of rest and activity may occur as you learn to repattern your sleep.

Use discretion; discover your optimal regime for good health and performance, and respect those needs in your daily routine. Then when situations arise that demand long periods of alert wakefulness, or that permit only intermittent catnaps, you will have available a powerful tool to carry you through safely and dependably.

Exercise — Going to Sleep

This exercise builds upon the relaxation process you learned in the previous chapter, extending it gently and smoothly into a deep, natural sleep.

1. Prepare yourself for rest.
2. Go through your physical and mental relaxation techniques, absorbing the peace and quietness of your passive fancy. Feel the warmth and heaviness of your body, the calmness and serenity of your mind, as you release all tension and cares.
3. Now imagine yourself walking to a delicate spiral staircase, leading clockwise downward from your peaceful scene. The staircase is enclosed in a crystal cylinder, light and airy. Outside the cylinder you see flowers and birds, clouds and treetops.
4. As you begin to descend the staircase, a chime sounds a musical note, a lighted number "100" appears, and a soft voice whispers, "Deeper".
5. You move slowly down the staircase, completing one turn of the spiral.

6. The chime sounds again, a lighted number "99" appears, and the voice murmurs, "Deeper".
7. You continue down the spiral, breathing the scented air, pausing at each level as the chime intones. The next descending number glows, and the hushed voice lulls you deeper.
8. As this continues, you drift gently and sweetly into sleep.

Exercise — Awakening

This process will teach you to awaken at any time you choose, without having to rely upon an alarm clock. While learning the technique, you might wish to take extra precautions to insure sound rest and peace of mind.

Set your alarm clock for the time you normally arise, but program yourself to awaken ten minutes earlier. You will sleep naturally and deeply, free from any concern of oversleeping, and will awaken at your designated time, ten minutes before the alarm sounds.

1. Enter your meditative level just before going to sleep.
2. Mentally tell your inner mind that you will awaken at the specific time, that you will be alert and fully refreshed upon arising.
3. Visualize a clock with the hands set at the desired time of awakening. Hold the visualization until you have a clear impression.
4. Gently release the image of the clock and drift into sleep.

You will wake up suddenly and completely at the exact moment you programmed before going to sleep.

Exercise — Staying Awake

This procedure is helpful to use occasionally when you are drowsy but wish to be awake and alert. *It is not intended to be a substitute for regular sleep*.
1. Take a few moments to drop down into your meditative level.

2. Inform your inner self, "I am going to sleep, I will have a full eight hours' rest, and I will open my eyes and be wide awake at _____ (designate a time 5 or 10 minutes later than now). I will be refreshed and alert and will stay refreshed and alert until I am ready to go to bed for my normal sleep."

3. Repeat again if you feel this will help program your inner mind effectively.

4. You will drift quickly into sleep, will rest deeply, and will open your eyes in five or ten minutes, feeling as revitalized as if you had actually been resting for several hours.

                    * * * * * * * * * * * * * * * * * * *

Since there is no time at the inner dimension, your mind and body will accept your directions and rejuvenate themselves almost as thoroughly as they would with a longer period of sleep.

As previously mentioned, learning to control your sleeping habits is the beginning of a new rapport between your outer and inner minds. Moreover, as this communion deepens, your sleeping habits will benefit, reflecting greater serenity and harmony in both waking and rest.

This will be true of all of these exercises and goals you accomplish successfully. Since you are an integrated being, the mastery of any one aspect of your personality will strengthen and reinforce all the others. As you attune to the inner realm, you will be learning to master your life with superconscious wisdom.

SECTION II
TAKING CHARGE

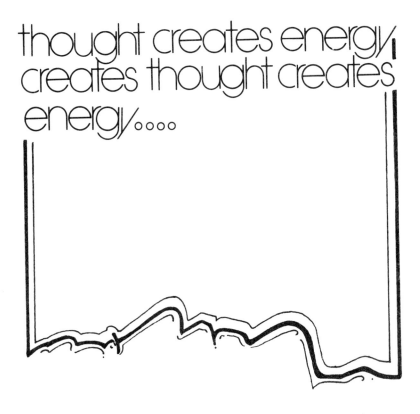

thoughts are creative; energy follows thought; thoughts
are energy . . .

CHAPTER 5
THE POWER OF THOUGHT

I n previous chapters you have been learning to choose and direct your thoughts. Your relaxation and sleep control techniques demonstrate that such voluntary control is possible, and that the methods for attaining this control are pleasant and readily learned. However, do not let the simplicity of the techniques and their ease of accomplishment minimize the magnitude of what you are doing. Learning to master your thinking is possibly the most important and vitally essential venture you can undertake.

Through your thoughts you create. With this great gift of creative thinking you are able to mold your life and to determine your destiny. At this very moment, whether you realize it or not, you are creating your future.

Your life today is the direct result of your previous and present thoughts, desires and emotions. Because of the creative power residing within your thoughts, you are solely responsible for all that happens to you. Your world is in a continual state of flux: malleable, changeable, forming and reforming, responsive to your every whim.

What a wonderful sense of freedom and rightness you will feel when you grasp the full import of these sentences! Once you understand that you alone have caused everything occurring in your life, you realize also that you have the power to correct any condition you wish by merely changing your thoughts.

Thoughts are Energy

The creative quality of thought is possible because of the fundamental interrelationship between consciousness, energy, and matter. Essentially, both matter and thought are forms of energy, operating at different frequencies of vibration.

You are probably familiar with the hypotheses of modern physics that propose energy as the foundation of material existence. Although the mechanics are not fully understood, energy differentiates into subatomic particles that compose atoms, which in turn create the building blocks of the material universe.

Thoughts also are energy, originating at a frequency too refined for scientific instruments to detect, but impinging upon the electromagnetic spectrum which embraces matter. Moreover, thoughts are magnetic, returning unerringly to the source from which they are sent.

It is not necessary to understand the precise ways in which consciousness, matter and energy equate; this is the subject of much metaphysical and parapsychological speculation. What *is* important is that you realize the creative and magnetic nature of thought and your ability to affect the world of matter through your mind. Let us explore further the behavior of thought as energy.

When you think a thought, it is projected far into the universe on its own individual wave-length or rate of vibration. It attracts to itself energy of the same vibration, tnen returns to you multiplied and magnified many times. This energy remains with you, forming a vortex which continues to magnetize to itself further energy of the same vibration.

You are an electro-magnetic being, surrounded by an electro-magnetic field which can be measured and seen. The exact colors and composition of this magnetic field are determined by the level of vibratory energy which you attract. Within this energy sphere the seeds of your thoughts are incubated to mature and blossom into your life's experiences. For all things are created first on the inner subjective plane before materializing in the outer physical world.

This principle is one of the basic laws of the spiritual dimension, stated repeatedly in esoteric literature:

"As a man thinketh in his heart, so is he." (Proverbs 23:7)

"As ye sow, so shall ye also reap." (Galations 6:7)

Thoughts and the Caliber of your Existence

Since all things in your life originate in your thoughts, the caliber of your existence is determined by the quality of your thoughts, by the vibratory level to which you attune.

As an analogy, whenever you set your television to a chosen channel, you align yourself to the frequency of that channel, and this becomes your viewing world. You exclude all other frequencies, even though they abound around you. In a like manner, you align yourself with a specific frequency when you select your level of thought, and that level becomes your actual reality.

If you indulge in fantasies of manipulation and control, such plotting will magnetize to you individuals who will attempt to manipulate you. If you project thoughts of suspicion or distrust and attempt to take advantage of people, you will live in an uneasy world in which others take advantage of you. Should you send forth feelings of anger, resentment and hostility, you will become ensnared in a backlash of anger and hostility directed to you.

Those who attune themselves to channels of lower vibrations, such as witchcraft or black magic, are subject to the laws of these levels. In this very real dimension, persons who study and practice these dark techniques become vulnerable to manipulation from others using the same processes. Meeting power with power, they find themselves in a constant struggle for control.

On the other hand, if you direct your attention to loftier goals, and have no interest or concern with the realms of darkness, you draw a mantle of protection around you. Higher rates of vibration negate the influences of any lower levels. The powers of light always overcome the lesser powers of darkness.

If you radiate feelings and thoughts of compassion and love, you can create with your mind your own personal paradise on earth. You will find yourself in a harmonious and supportive environment, meeting only kindly, benevolent people. Love will return to you multifold.

Research in the Influence of Thought

Once you become aware of the creative power of thought, you can observe its action in your own life and in the lives of others. Its ramifications can also be demonstrated objectively through the studies and experiments of psychological and parapsychological research. For example:

Biofeedback equipment and electro-encephalograph (EEG) instruments record the minute electrical energy which emanates from the brain, measuring precisely the fluctuations and changes of a subject's thinking. As he alters his states of consciousness, these instruments will show his exact levels of awareness.

When he is using his logical, rational mind, the energy will be indicated on an oscilloscope as a line which undulates at a rapid, shallow rate, peaking between 14 and 21 times per second. This level of awareness is called the "beta" level.

When a subject relaxes into a meditative state, his brain activity will diminish, showing a rhythm of 7 to 14 cycles per second. This level of consciousness, which is the one you are now learning to manifest, is called the "alpha" level.

A still slower rhythm of 4 to 7 cycles per second indicates the "theta" level of awareness, a state seldom experienced consciously by the average person. This is the level of very deep meditation, the level to which a clinical hypnotist will guide clients to induce anaesthesia; it is the level we reach in sudden emergencies when we react instinctively and correctly.

The "delta" level of consciousness is registered as a very slow rhythm from 1/2 to 4 cycles per second. This is the level of the deep unconscious, or coma.

For centuries mystical seekers have been aware of the reality and nature of these differing levels of thought, using various terms to differentiate and describe them. Now there are instruments which measure and classify these mind levels. Through these instruments we can actually determine whether a subject is attuned to his outer self or to his inner self.

When he is using his rational, reasoning capabilities, the activity of the left hemisphere of the brain predominates, while his intuitive, introspective thinking usually originates on the right side of the brain.

Thoughts Made Visible

Results of thinking and feeling are recorded in a different way through Kirlian Photography (electro-photography), using special techniques to photograph the energy field, or aura, surrounding the body. In radiant designs of color and brilliance, patterns which swirl and flow, the changing medleys of one's thoughts are beautifully captured on film.

Perhaps the most dramatic evidence of the reality of thoughts and emotions is to observe those changes personally by extending your visual range to finer vibrations, and learning to see auras. Students of parapsychology who develop this ability are able to witness fascinating panoramas of color and light which faithfully record the slightest variations in their subject's thinking.

Negative thoughts and emotions are perceived as dark, murky colors, while positive feelings and thoughts are brilliant and clear. Advanced students can actually see images, or thought-forms begin to develop in the aura as a subject concentrates his attention strongly upon an idea or visualization.

The Power of Words

Words are almost as powerful as thoughts. Since that which you send forth returns to you magnified and intensified, the words which you speak have a profound effect upon your own life and upon the lives of others. The impact of your thoughts increases greatly when you express those thoughts in words, for you are concentrating and focusing their power.

Words, however, have an additional characteristic of far greater importance: when you speak, you are not only communicating with other people, you are also giving commands to yourself.

Your inner self is a willing servant, eager to comply with any directives you give. Through your thoughts and spoken words, you are continuously issuing those directives. Your off-hand remarks, your casual conversation, your private musings, as well as your most profound proclamations are all noted and recorded by your cooperative lower self. Those expressions you voice repeatedly, with emotion or with emphasis, make a deep impression upon the inner mind, which will invariably put them into effect.

If you listen to average conversations with a critical ear, you will probably be surprised to hear a preponderance of negative conditioning. You may be able to discern a remarkable correlation between the problems of the speakers and the thoughts they are expressing.

Ask yourself, "What type of directives am I giving to my inner mind and do I really mean what I am saying?"

Words Which Can Create Problems

Some phrases should be eliminated entirely from your vocabulary, for they subtly impose unnecessary limitations.

Such phrases include:
"I can't . . ."
"I'll never be able to . . ."
"I always . . ."
"I never . . ."
"I forgot . . ."
"It's no use . . ."
"I'm trying to . . ." (instead of "I'm doing . . .")

Whenever you inform your subconscious mind of shortcomings, you nullify your true capabilities, for your inner mind will faithfully erect the barriers you specify.

If you assert that certain things make you angry or nervous or upset, you may wonder why you find yourself suddenly and unaccountably angry or nervous when exposed to these conditions. Although your attention is directed elsewhere, and you are completely unaware of the triggering circumstances, your inner mind has learned its lesson and is capably carrying out your stated wishes.

Thus the phrases and the figures of speech which you use habitually may actually be the source of unwanted problems in your life. Remember that your inner mind literally accepts any expression such as these which you use unthinkingly:

"School is a pain in the neck."
"I'm breaking my back to get this done."
"It makes my blood boil."
"You make me sick."
"It just kills me!"
"I'm tickled to death."
"I'm sick and tired of this."
"I'm just worn out trying to get this done."
"It makes my heart ache . . . I'm heartbroken."
"I'll never be able to digest all of this."
"It takes my breath away."
"I can't swallow that."
"I'd cut my throat first."
"Oh my aching back!"

If you frequently use expletives such as "I'll be damned!",

"Go to Hell", or "The devil with it", you may well think about replacing them with more benevolent utterances. Since these phrases are really just habits, why not take advantage of an excellent opportunity to accrue a few extra blessings?

Used with the same intonation, you can express your mood just as effectively with "I'll be blessed!", "Heavenly days!", or "Good Heavens!", and others of like nature. Who knows what may happen?

Proclamations of failure are self-fulfilling. You will miss your plane, fail your tests, or court disaster in your ventures if you so program yourself. Therefore, do not use terms of foreboding or expectations of non-success, such as:

"I just know I won't get there on time."

"This old car will break down before we've gone 10 miles."

"Things just never work out right for me."

Words, Thoughts, Aging and Health

Your thoughts, your words and your expectations can have a pronounced effect upon your rate of aging. You can be catapulted into old age if you believe that accumulative years automatically bring debility and decrease in competence.

Rapid aging seems to follow specific birthdays for many people, who feel that forty or fifty are landmark ages, or that their value to society ceases with their sixty-fifth birthday. As they accept with resignation the limitations which they believe accompanies specific ages, we often hear remarks like those which compound the effects of their thoughts:

"I'm too old for that."

"You can't teach an old dog new tricks."

"Us old folks."

"Be your age."

"I can't expect to do that at my age."

Wide variations in the aging process occur in different cultures and families, as do attitudes towards age. Perhaps our heritage of expectations and emotions about growing older is even more important than the physical tendencies our ancestors bequeath to us.

In health also, our thoughts, words and imaginations play major roles. By our thinking alone we can make ourselves ill. Through their fears, hypochondriacs tend to attract symptoms of currently popular illnesses, while medical students traditionally convince themselves that they are beset in turn with every malady they study.

When we review our "operations" or recount the complications of past sicknesses, we are retaining or recreating within our energy fields the same destructive forces which were present in the original condition, and which can manifest again in the same or similar ways.

Not only regarding health, but from every other standpoint, optimum living requires that you focus your attention and the creative power of your thoughts and words upon the present. By reactivating memories and past emotions, you recreate your history, and relive the same situations again and again. If you nurse past grievances or dwell upon the injustices and problems of the past, you draw those same issues to yourself in the future.

The person you are today is a composite of everything you have ever been. . . . you have already assimilated the lessons and experiences of previous times. Free yourself then from the burden of past regrets and mistakes; release them, let them go, and use the wisdom you have gained to create a more bountiful present and future.

To summarize, monitor your thoughts . . . attune to the highest and the best. Begin to watch your speech carefully. Remove from your thinking and conversations any concepts or expressions which might have even the slightest negative connotations. Replace them with positive ideas and statements, and program yourself for success, for happiness, for fulfillment. Your beautiful inner partner will follow your positive commands with the same precision and exactitude it exhibits with the negative. Thoughts have unlimited power, and words are crystallized thoughts.

CHAPTER 6
MODEL THE CHILD AND
YOU FORM THE ADULT

As you consider the importance of thoughts and words, you may not realize that another influence is helping to shape your mind and your life. This factor is the programming and conditioning you received as a child. It is so fundamental, such an integral part of you, that you may feel this is the true you; this is "just the way you are". Actually many of your basic attitudes and approaches to life were acquired during early childhood.

Children are deeply impressionable, for they must absorb from their environments the qualities and training required to survive and to function independently during later life.

From your parents and other individuals in your immediate environment, you learned your habits, your attitudes and your underlying responses to the challenges of life. Nature protected you during your most vulnerable years by making you totally receptive to the influences around you, allowing you to adapt to the unique requirements of your own individual world. As you grew in strength and ability, this blind acceptance was gradually replaced with self-direction.

This development is beautifully illustrated in the changing patterns of brain activity reflected in the octaves of growth a child experiences during the maturation process. Through biofeedback we learn that a child spends a large portion of his time from birth to 3 1/2 or 4 years of age in delta (1/2 to 3 1/2 or 4 cycles a second). From 4 years until age 7 or 8, he stays most of the time in theta (3 1/2 or 4 to 7 or 8 cycles per second).

From 7 or 8 years until he is 13 or 14, he lives mostly in the alpha level (7 or 8 cycles per second to 13 1/2 or 14). From puberty until his 21st year, an adolescent spends his waking hours predominately in beta, developing the logical, reasoning attributes of his mind. How fascinating that the octaves of years correspond almost exactly with the cycles of brain rhythm!

Thus we observe that children are in the intuitive, transformative levels of consciousness most of the time. A little child accepts as truth all that is told him, for reasoning and discrimination come with maturity.

From studies in age regression, we discover that even a fetus is sensitive to the emotions, thoughts and words of both parents, and to the influences of the world around it. Acutely sensitive to the flow of feelings in his surroundings, a baby learns success or failure before leaving the crib. He is functioning in the deepest survival level, forming the basic foundation for the structure of his life.

Parental Programming

We program our children constantly, with corrections, discussions, directives, and especially with examples. Thus it is that you, programmed by your own parents, are living out that conditioning.

Unfortunately, the tendency of parents is to program their children negatively, for they were so programmed by their parents. . . . who in turn were programmed negatively by their parents, ad infinitum. Parents find themselves perpetuating the attitudes and habits which were impressed upon them during their own formative years. They treat their children as they themselves were treated while they were growing up, even though they may have rebelled against that treatment at the time. Generation after generation the same mistakes may be propagated if nothing is done to break the cycle.

Now, however, we are learning to alter this process at its roots. Through many types of psychotherapy we are discovering the influences and experiences of youth which shaped the problems appearing in our adult lives.

From the opposite direction, we are studying the nature of childhood in ever more sophisticated ways, using our findings to develop more compassionate and constructive methods of child-rearing. As we grow in understanding, we are attempting to undo the mistakes of the past, and to give our children more loving, supportive care.

This progress is not universally known, however. You need only listen to any group of parents with their children, to hear the negative programming which is still being poured into the minds of children. Or you may listen to children playing, and hear repeated verbatim the parental injunctions already assimilated into their beings.

You will hear repeatedly such statements as these, and you will probably shudder to realize that they are being accepted as literal truths:

"If you sit in a draft you will catch cold."

"Your shoes are soaking wet! You will catch pneumonia sure as anything."

"Don't climb so high! You will fall and break your neck."

"Don't eat that. . . . it will make you sick.

"You will never be able to do that. Why do you try?"

"You never can do anything right."

"You are a bad boy. . . . or a wicked girl."

"How can you be so stupid? (or lazy or dumb, or selfish, or clumsy . . .)

With such thoughtless phrases, undesirable qualities are planted into completely open little minds. Deeply instilled is the conviction that they really are stupid or lazy or incorrigible, that they are prone to sickness or injury — beliefs which persist as psy-pathological blocks throughout their lifetimes.

How many diseases or tendencies toward disease are actually hereditary — how many are programmed during childhood? Allergies may result from watching a parent sneezing uncontrollably while reviling the culprit blooms and grasses he feels to be responsible for his discomfort. If warned that particular foods are indigestible, that certain actions will result in injury or sickness, a child may carry out such programming and fulfill those dire predictions throughout his childhood and adult life.

Negative Influences, Detection

As you become increasingly aware of the impact of negative influences upon your life, you will also become increasingly adept at detecting their presence in your surroundings. You will probably be startled to discover how negative our society tends to be.

The news media bring the violence, the tragedies, and the unhappiness of the entire world into the privacy of your home, while seldom reporting the triumphs, the happiness and the joys which equally abound. Television, books, plays, films, and most conversations dwell upon the foibles and shortcomings of human existence, overlooking inspirational and praiseworthy happenings.

With your accelerating growth in consciousness, it is important to protect yourself from the destructive impact of this flood of negativity. Since your inner mind is accepting all to which it is exposed, and preserving it carefully in your memory, this becomes the raw material from which your individual universe is being formed.

Vicarious experiences will condition your future as powerfully as actual events, for your Lesser Self lacks the ability to distinguish the difference. Therefore, be highly selective of the books you read, the plays, television programs and movies you watch, as well as the events of the world to which you direct your attention.

Be especially careful with films and television, for while

you are absorbed in watching them you are particularly receptive to suggestion. As you become engrossed in a scene, you drop into a meditative state, almost a comatose stupor, during which everything you see and hear is deeply impressed.

This condition is but a temporary enchantment for adults, but children are far more vulnerable. They are in the most highly suggestible states of awareness almost all of the time, are forming the fundamental precepts upon which they will govern their lives, and have not yet developed the ability to evaluate the material to which they are exposed.

Into the mental reservoirs from which you and your children are creating your future, are being channeled turmoil, distress, moral laxity, and graphic descriptions of physical ailments. The headaches, upset stomachs, aching backs and stuffy noses which can follow attentive viewing are of minor concern compared to the more serious consequences resulting from focusing your mind upon the more sordid aspects of living.

Negative Influences, Protection

How do you protect yourself against such a sea of negativity? Your understanding of the forces and issues involved is already giving you a decided advantage in neutralizing their impact. Now practice the following steps, which will effectively counteract negativity and create a positive magnetic field around you.

1. Begin by becoming aware of the negative influences in your environment and deciding that you will no longer accept them.
2. Program your inner mind to reject all negative thoughts.
3. Remind yourself that you are totally protected from harm at all times.
4. Monitor your thoughts and words, firmly eliminating all negative ideas and expressions.

5. Program a key word or phrase to eliminate negativity (see description below).
6. Be discriminating in selecting the books, newspapers and magazines you read, the movies and television shows you watch.
7. Seek the companionship of people with positive, optimistic viewpoints, those who uplift and inspire you.
8. Focus your thoughts and attention upon the positive and beautiful in life. Plan for and expect only the best to come to you.

Program a key word or phrase as a cue to instruct your inner mind to cancel any negativity which comes in your direction, and use that cue any time you are exposed to detrimental environments or unaware people.

For example, while you are in your deep meditative level of awareness you can suggest to your inner self that the words "cancel" or "clear", expressed aloud or to yourself, will repel any negativity. Or you can select a word which reduces the influence of such negativity to nothing, a word such as "zero". But the most convenient word, one which means the same as zero, is "oh". You can use it with varying intonations, as an interjection, an explanation, or comment during conversation, and your cooperative inner self will efficiently shield you from the negative thoughts and speech around you.

You will find that the results of these suggestions are surprisingly quick and gratifying. Within a very short time you will no longer be expressing negative thoughts or emotions, and will automatically reject any which come to you from others. You will express only positive ideas, and in so doing will have a profoundly beneficient effect not only upon your own being, but upon others whom you encounter.

You have been learning ways of protecting yourself against destructive influences, and ways of attracting constructive influences to yourself. Extend the same precautions and considerations into your relationships with other people, for your thoughts, words and attitudes have far-reaching impact upon the lives of others as well as upon your own. Be especially gentle with other people's hopes and plans. When someone asks your opinion of an undertaking, respond with enthusiasm, even though you may harbor private reservations. Help his imagination to soar, discuss with him the possibilities, let the ideas flourish and grow. The obstacles and shortcomings will become apparent as you plan. In the positive environment you have helped create, he will discover ways to overcome the challenges and drawbacks, or will dismiss the idea as impractical. You will both feel a glow of accomplishment from a shared venture, rather than dejection and disgruntlement from a suppressed vision. Your thoughts and your words have nurtured his ability to dream.

As you observe the power of thought operating in your life, you will find convincing illustrations of the truth that you create with your mind. Wherever you focus your attention, you magnetize those influences and experiences into your universe.

So determine then to give the precious power of your interest and attention only to those things which are constructive. . . . to the beautiful, the wholesome, the joyous and bountiful. All things of a lesser nature will miraculously disappear, as the consummate world your thoughts conjure is first impressed upon the higher planes, and then manifested as your reality.

CHAPTER 7
CREATING YOUR INNER
WORKSHOP

Now that you have learned to relax and enter deeper levels at will, and have begun to consider the reality and power of thought, you are ready to create a workshop on the inner dimensions. This is a very special place you will use for all subsequent processes. It will serve as a refuge of security and rejuvenation, a center of guidance, healing and inspiration. It is yours alone, a private kingdom where you may work and create with absolute sovereignty, whenever you wish.

Exercise — Creating your Inner Workshop

1. Enter your meditative level with the method you have been using. You should reach this basic working level comfortably, easily and quickly.
2. Imagine a staircase ascending upward to a doorway.
3. Begin to walk slowly up the stairs, counting backward with each step from 15 to 1. Feel yourself rising higher with each step.
4. When you reach the top step, at stair #1, pause before the door. Then open it and step inside.
5. You are now within a room, a beautiful chamber which you will redesign and decorate. Give your imagination free rein, be innovative, and design your room to include everything you desire. You may want a fountain, a grand piano, a swimming pool, a waterfall — anything at all.

You may place your room wherever you wish; in the mountains, under the ocean, out in space. Remember, this is your estate, your inner palace, and on these interior planes your choices are unlimited.

6. Leave one wall free, on the south side, for special additions which you will install later.
7. Place three chairs facing the south wall; one in the middle for yourself, and seats on either side for guests whom you will invite in a later exercise.
8. Include a clock and a perpetual calendar.
9. Create an information center, such as a library or a computer, which will contain all the knowledge you wish to have.
10. Create a screen, the size of a movie screen, which can be pulled down on your south wall. The screen is high on the wall; as you view it you raise your eyes upward about 20 degrees.
11. Spend as much time as you wish to create the workshop of your dreams.
12. When you feel that your workshop is complete, open the door to the stairway, descend the stairs, counting each step from 1 to 15.
13. Return to your basic meditative level, then bring yourself to waking consciousness in the usual manner.

Return to your inner workshop frequently as you relax and meditate, altering it in any way whenever you wish. When your workshop feels very real and you can reach it quickly in meditation, you will be ready to add other features which will enable you to send healing on the inner planes. These innovations will be discussed in the chapter on healing.

Many people see other people's workshops, but usually because they have a close personal relationship, or a specific reason for being there. Since your workshop is your private domain, you have complete autonomy and may admit or refuse anyone you choose.

Your workshop is a very real place, which actually exists

on the etheric plane. We have discussed the creative power of thought; now you have produced a tangible creation which becomes more concrete each time you think of it.

Whenever you enter your workshop, you will immediately feel that you are in a special, sanctified space, a retreat for renewal and inspiration as well as for projects and learning. Use it whenever you meditate; it will soon become your personal sanctuary, intimate and pristine. From this base of inner security, you are well prepared to manifest your personal goals and to send forth your light and love into the world.

. . . we channel wisdom from a higher intelligence and learn as we teach . . .

CHAPTER 8
INNER LEARNING

The art of learning will prove invaluable to you as you progress on the pathway to self-mastery. Moreover, it is immeasurably useful in the pragmatics of daily life. As you perfect the techniques of self-education that are presented in this chapter, you will enrich your life in a far greater way than you can imagine.

While the psychology of learning is a broad field which has attracted a good deal of research and attention in recent decades, your approach to learning will differ markedly from traditional methods of instruction. Instead of the customary disciplines of rigorous study and rote memory, you will utilize the powers of your mind to bypass the ingrained barriers to knowledge and discovery. You will develop techniques to instantly recall information stored in your memory, and then you will learn to receive knowledge directly through inspiration and intuition.

You have the unlimited power of genius — right now — though it probably remains largely untapped because your mind's capacity is only partly utilized. You will now enlarge the functional capability of your lower mind and access its data banks as efficiently as a computer retrieves its programs. But you will do far more than any machine, for you can originate and create totally new designs, and integrate them into the overview of your universal reality.

We have discussed the power of thought, yet most of us forget the impact and importance of every single idea and notion that passes through our minds. The most idle, wistful fantasy, the tiniest flicker of emotion, are recorded indelibly upon the easel of eternity. For thought, as energy, is impressed irrevocably in the archives of the Universe.

Since time (as we understand it) does not exist on the inner dimension, the immense accumulation of all humanity's thoughts — past, present and future — comprise a great storehouse of knowledge and wisdom. The depths of tragedy and human depravity are recorded, as well as the grandeur and profundity of the ages. Proper use of the techniques given in this book, employed with sincerity and the desire to serve, will enable you to avoid the negative thought-forms of the human race and reap only that wisdom which will benefit you.

Human intelligence is but one component of Universal Intelligence, wherein all things are known; omniscience is the attribute of the illuminated mind. Once you have learned to reach beyond your own mind and attune to Universal Wisdom, you will establish a permanent source of creativity, inspiration, intuition and inner guidance.

The techniques you will use to reach this point are seemingly simple, for they are merely awakening that which you already possess. You are not becoming brighter nor more of a genius; you are actually allowing that faculty of your being to express itself more fully. In so doing, you are opening the doors to your own infinite perfection.

The Key to Exceptional Learning

The key to exceptional learning ability is concentration, or the power to discipline your thoughts. Normally, the energy which flows through your mind is random, a diffused pattern of concentric ripples similar to the waves formed when a stone is dropped into a still pool. In these exercises, you will focus your mind's energy like a laser beam, with pinpoint accuracy and precision.

In the last chapter, you created a screen inside your workshop for viewing some of the exercises you will be doing. This screen serves as a boundary or frame in which to confine and focus your thoughts.

In most exercises you will be asked to visualize images. The ability to visualize mentally varies among individuals; approximately 60% of the population tends to actually see images (known as clairvoyance), while the remainder senses or feels impressions rather than seeing them. Any mode of perception is acceptable, for it is your predominate way of imaging. As you work with these methods you will become more adept at all modes, but accept the way that comes easiest for you as a personal propensity.

Programming a Cue

You will also learn to attune yourself immediately to your inner screen. This is accomplished by means of a "cue", a preprogrammed signal to your inner mind that instructs it to attune your consciousness to your creative level and to activate the inner screen. Any cue you select would be effective, but we are going to program one which has been used by many esoteric disciplines for millenia.

This cue is created by forming a circle with the thumb and forefinger of either (or both) hand(s). You may also choose to use the thumb and both the index and middle fingers. In either case, your hand will fall into this position easily and naturally, and maintain it comfortably for a period of time.

This cue is used for a definite reason. Most of the time a great stream of energy flows through your fingertips. By putting the fingertips together, the energy flow is recycled back into your body, concentrating it for added power in your mental visualization and inner work. For this reason, many Eastern spiritual studies have used this cue to aid in meditation and contemplation; you will use it now for problem-solving and inner development.

Because our minds are constantly bombarded by an incredible barrage of sensations, information and ideas, the inner mind filters this input. It stores into short-term, accessible memory only that information which is impressed strongly by repetition, emotional intensity or fervent desire. However, experiments in age regression indicate that *all* mental input is actually stored permanently in long-term memory. Usually this information is not readily accessible, but with the cooperation of your inner mind you may draw out any memory you desire. You may also communicate with your inner mind to record specific information for easy retrieval at a later time.

The following exercises outline procedures to be used in learning and memorizing. They are useful for anyone wishing to improve his learning skills, although they may seem to be directed especially to students.

Exercise

1. Relax and enter your meditative, creative level.
2. Inform your inner mind that you are preparing to read a book or listen to a lecture.
3. Instruct your inner mind that you may recall this information at any time by simply placing your thumb and forefingers together in the cue described earlier.
4. Allow your inner mind to classify the material by giving the following information:
   (a) Title of book, article or lecture;
   (b) Name of author or lecturer;
   (c) Date of reading or lecture;
   (d) Anything else which will help to classify the material to be learned.
5. Open your eyes and read the book or listen to the lecture.
6. Upon completion of the reading or listening to the speaker, re-enter your meditative level and repeat the instructions given in steps 3 and 4.
7. When the need arises, you will be able to recall any or all of the material programmed previously.

* * * * * * * * * * * * * * * * * * * *

If you have a large volume of facts to memorize, go

through the steps above, then read the material a second time. Pay particular attention to the specific ideas or facts you wish to remember. For added effectiveness, make a cassette recording of the information to be learned. You can then sit in a comfortable, relaxed position, undistracted by any activity, and listen to your tape.

You may need to listen to the tape more than once for total recall, especially when you are just beginning to work with this approach. This technique will impress the information deeply into your memory and make it easy to recollect whenever you need.

Many people enjoy listening to music while their memory tape is playing quietly in the background. This is a delightfully effortless way to learn, but requires selective discrimination in the type of music played.

Some music will undermine concentration; rock music, for example, dissipates energy and interrupts the thinking processes. Choose peaceful music conducive to reflection and repose. Some classical music, such as Baroque pieces, enhance learning for many people. An entire new genre of "celestial" or "New Age" music has been composed in recent years specifically for its relaxing, soothing effect on the human psyche. Some personal experimentation will determine which music is best to use for your own study aid.

Expect to have immediate results as you work with these techniques, for they are surprisingly effective. Students are usually able to select ahead of time the grades they wish to receive, and to produce the quality of performance that will warrant those grades.

When you have studied your lesson material using the methods outlined, you are ready to learn the following method of taking examinations:

Exercise — Taking Examinations

A. *Pre-test*
1. Meditate a short time upon entering the test area to put

yourself into a relaxed, tranquil state of mind.
2. Once you have reached your creative level, visualize yourself on your inner visual screen.
3. See yourself confident, knowledgeable, answering all the questions correctly.
4. Then change the scene and visualize yourself happily receiving your corrected examination paper marked with the grade you desire.
5. When you open your eyes, you will be relaxed and positively expectant, ready to begin your test.

B. *During the Examination*
1. Read the first question. If an answer occurs easily, with no doubt or uncertainty, write it down. If no answer comes clearly, skip the first question and proceed to the next.
2. Continue through all the test questions, answering only those you know with certainty and leaving the rest blank.
3. When you have gone through the entire test in this manner, return to the questions which you initially omitted.
4. Close your eyes, cue your mind with your fingertips together, and mentally repeat the question. If no answer comes to mind, go on to the next unanswered question. Proceed through the test in this manner.
   Do not second-guess yourself!
5. (You will be meeting your spiritual guides in a later chapter, so you may postpone this step for test-taking until then.) If any questions remain unanswered at the end of step 4, deepen your meditative level by counting backwards from 25 to 1. This will place you in a quiet inner space where you can draw upon your spiritual guides for assistance. Ask your guides the questions you need, and the answers they give will be correct.
6. If there are still any unanswered questions, you may try this final technique (which may seem far-fetched until you actually use it). Enter a deep meditative level, by

counting backwards from 25 to 1, then project the image of your instructor onto your mental screen. When you have a clear impression of the teacher, simply ask him the question. He will reply with the correct answer. His response will express his personality unmistakably, as if you were speaking with him in person on the outer level.

* *

It is important that you accept the first answer which comes to you when you use these techniques. This first, usually immediate response originates from the intuitive level, and is accurate. If you refuse to acknowledge this serendipitous answer, preferring instead to question and analyze, you are reacting from the logical, reasoning mind, and will be restricted to its limitations.

Very little practice is required to master these learning techniques, giving you a most valuable skill. Imagine the applications and ramifications of such a talent when applied to the situations of your life! As you utilize these processes, you will rekindle the joy and thrill of learning. No longer will you feel trapped by hours of arduous, tedious labor; you will soar with the stimulating excitement of growth and discovery.

CHAPTER 9
RESOLVING PROBLEMS

I n the preceding chapter you were introduced to more effective ways of learning about your external environment, methods for mastering scholastic and academic skills. Now you will direct your attention to an even more exciting and pertinent type of education: learning to solve the problems and surmount the obstacles of your own life. Through perfecting your imagination and applying special techniques of visualization, you will begin to recognize your problems for what they really are — challenges and training opportunities to further your own self-mastery.

The method you will use for resolving problems is based upon the understanding that the lower mind is highly cooperative when approached on the level upon which it operates. By relaxing deeply and using pictorial images, you can consciously "reprogram" your lower mind to accept and act upon any suggestion you choose. Since your lower self has been programmed from birth with countless myths and mistaken beliefs, it is best to first remove previous conditioning before presenting new suggestions. It is wise also to study the problem from the intuitive level before instituting changes.

The basic process may seem simple, however the applications are limitless. Not only will you learn the method quickly, with immediate results, but you will find the techniques themselves engrossing and fun.

Exercise — Changing the Frame of Your Life

1. Select an issue in your life which you would like to change.
2. Relax and enter your meditative level.
3. Imagine your inner visual screen, then enclose it in a black frame.
4. Project an image of your problem onto your screen, seeing it either symbolically or as it actually appears in your life.

Think of all the ramifications of the problem, exaggerating, examining, scrutinizing every condition and detail. You are designating to your inner mind those aspects you wish to change, so take your time.

5. When you have made a comprehensive and complete study of the problem, erase the images from the screen. Feel all of the emotions associated with the pictures washed away as well.
6. Tell yourself that you will never again think about the problem as you had previously considered it. As you release the images and feelings, mentally vow that they will never enter your world again.
7. Now imagine the frame which surrounds your screen changing to clear, shining white.
8. Project onto the white-framed screen images which depict the solution to your problem. Again, you may visualize symbolically.
9. Allow the answers to flow spontaneously, for at this level you are attuning to a higher guidance than that which your normal thoughts perceive.
10. Let feelings of happiness and rightness accompany the images. Immerse yourself in the event as totally as if you were truly living it, full of expectancy and the satisfaction you will feel when it actually comes to pass.
11. Take your time to savor the glow of fulfillment, the balm of success. Consider the opportunities which will open,

the benefits and advantages you will enjoy, the effects on all those involved. Let everyone win.

12. When you have experienced your solution fully, erase the scene from your visual screen, release it and let it go.
13. Give thanks, knowing that the project has been accomplished. Tell yourself that from now on you will think of the situation only in terms of this new solution, in terms of success.
14. Repeat your visualization of the solution as you saw it on the white-framed screen as often as you wish, for each repetition will draw added energy to aid in manifestation. This is a thoroughly proven, effective technique, so expect your requests to be granted.

* * * * * * * * * * * * * * * * * * * *

When you visualize in this exercise, you are actually creating forms of the imaged solution on the inner planes. A clairvoyant will be able to see them clearly visible in your energy field. Because all things are composed of energy, visualization can transmute your desires from wishful thinking into physical reality.

With the creative power of your thoughts, you mold the essence of the universe, transforming it into the slower vibrations of matter. It is perfectly possible to create everything you could feasibly wish or desire. Your only limitations are your own expectations.

Those things which are to manifest on the inner subjective planes will occur immediately, but those which are to appear on the material plane may require a little more time, as materialization on this plane utilizes more energy. Nonetheless, trust that the inner reality already exists, seeking expression in outward form.

Outreach

You will naturally use these techniques first on the most pressing problems in your own life. Once they have been resolved, you will probably turn your attention to the affairs of your family and friends. You may proceed with great fervor to quietly and inconspicuously aid the reorganization of their worlds into greater harmony and richness. Many of the solutions which you program for their problems will prove most satisfactory, but sooner or later you will encounter an experience which forcibly brings home to you the realization that in this instance it would have been better had you not interfered.

This experience pinpoints an important lesson: there is one further step in creative programming which is perhaps the major requirement for success. This step is the essential one of turning all decisions and results over to Higher Consciousness.

When we program with affirmations and visualizations, we are working with our conscious logical minds to direct our emotional lower selves. However, these limited aspects of our Beings don't always know the best solution to a problem. It is essential to enlist the guidance and infinite intelligence of our High Selves if we are to produce results which are for the highest good of all concerned.

Hence the final step in programming is to turn the resolution of the problem over to your Higher Self or to the greater wisdom of the Universe. It may help to use a phrase such as "This is what I ask if it be Thy will", or "May I receive this or better according to the perfect pattern of my life", or simply, "Thy will be done".

Then release your request, let it go, and give thanks in the perfect trust that all will be accomplished according to Higher Guidance.

Asking and Receiving

The solution to a problem resolved in this manner may arrive in a totally unexpected form, so be alert to the unimagined and unobtrusive. The deepest desires of your heart and soul will always be fulfilled as you request . . . or in a way far more exquisite, so attune yourself to that which you truly wish, in order to perceive the many blessings in disguise which are constantly flowing to you.

Prayers and Affirmations

Whenever you work with natural laws, with imaging and programming, praying and asking, little will be forthcoming until you release your requests and let them go. If you continue to worry, think and plan after you have asked for a solution on the inner planes, then you have not truly released and are still imprisoning the project within your own energy field.

You must loosen your hold on your petition, free it to go to the greater universe, if you are to enlist the assistance of Higher Guidance and Power. Only in this manner will your dreams expand beyond the narrow territory of your personal boundaries, to flower in the vast dimensions of a greater reality.

Law of Flow

One of the universal principles of abundance and manifestation is the law of flow. Basically, life is movement and continual change. When you are thriving, normal healthy activity causes a constant flow in all of your affairs. When you remove something from your life, it creates a vacuum which enables something else to flow to you. If you use the law of flow intelligently, you discard or give away those things which you no longer need or use, thereby creating a vacuum which will magnetize to you those things you need and desire now.

When you store away objects unused and unnoticed, the opposite condition occurs. Your energy is immobilized, causing a static condition which blocks the flow of the new into your life. So clean out your closets, empty your shelves, discover the pleasure of giving to others objects of value. You will bask in an aura of freedom and clarity — and create the optimum conditions for a quick response to your programming and visualizations.

Exactness

Another important principle is exactness. Be as specific as possible when you program your goals. Know what you want, and visualize it in detail. Study your objective thoroughly, until all specifications are clearly established in your mind. The sharper the image you present, the more energy you focus.

On the other hand, be sure that your vision is broad enough to encompass the best that could possibly happen. Always leave room for something better than your current expectation to occur, and give the Universe an opportunity to exceed the limitations of your present vision.

If you wish career advancement, for instance, you might picture yourself promoted in your current employment. A more open-ended approach, however, would be to see yourself employed in an occupation which is enjoyable, stimulating, demanding the best you can offer, and rewarding you with happiness and fulfillment in all ways.

The result of this more comprehensive approach could establish you in the first position you considered, or it could result in an offer from another source for a position with much greater scope and return.

Perhaps an opportunity in an entirely different field may appear unexpectedly. You might find yourself working with your hobbies or deepest interests, in an occupation more rewarding than anything you could have imagined. Visualize clearly, but leave open boundaries.

End Results

When you examine the projects you are expecting to manifest, set your sights on the ultimate goal. Program for the end-result rather than the intermediate steps.

For example, your project may be to acquire a new car. One method would be to see yourself receiving the necessary money and then shopping for just the right vehicle. A better approach would be to imagine yourself already owning the car you want, leaving the method of procurement to the Universe. Then perhaps you might win that exact car, it may be given to you, or in some way you might find yourself in possession of a far more luxurious model.

The possibilities are endless. Use your imagination to dream of results unfettered by the presumed demands of practicality or propriety. The results will be greater than you expect.

Laws of Manifestation

A very important law of manifestation involves ethics. One must never use his or her abilities to take advantage of another person. More than this, it is important to go beyond simply refraining from injury to an active desire for other people's greatest benefit.

For example, if you are programming to obtain a promotion to a specific new job, perhaps you could imagine at the same time that the person presently holding the desired position be promoted to another position which more fully satisfies his needs and desires.

It is probably unlikely that you could always know unerringly what is best for everyone involved when you fulfill your personal wishes. However, your goodwill and loving intention will bring positive benefit to all those concerned, and will return to you multiplied manyfold.

Fulfilling Desires

Whenever you have a strong desire for something, there is a valid reason behind it. Many spiritual paths have taught that the way to freedom from attachment to desires is to deny them constantly and resolutely until they wither away.

In our approach, which seems to be in harmony with the Age in which we are living and the predilections of our culture, we fulfill our desires in the most ethical, high-minded way possible. For in conscious fulfillment of current desires also comes the release and maturity needed for progress into greater and higher aspirations.

Depending upon your orientation, you may find that most of your desires at first are for material objects, for particular types of relationships with people, or for emotional qualities such as happiness and self-esteem.

As you succeed in fulfilling the desires in one area of your life, you will naturally begin to expand into previously neglected regions. You may discover a craving for more intellectual stimulation and enrichment, for more spiritual certitude and understanding. This is part of the normal path of personal awakening which occurs as a natural outgrowth of the development of your power to create and to receive the fruits of that creation.

When you finally realize that you actually do have the power and ability to materialize your dreams, a marked change of focus commences in your thinking and in the nature of your wishing. Your wishes become simplified — you now desire only those things and circumstances which are exactly right for you. You feel a deep need to be free from the burden and care of superfluous possessions and entanglements. Your life becomes streamlined and clarified.

Use your programming skills to manifest your heart's desire, to savor the pleasure of fulfilling your dreams. The path of self-discovery yields many surprises and unexpected benefactions.

CHAPTER 10
PROGRAMMING

You have now reached a special stage in your progress. You have received enough basic techniques to enable you to consciously direct and redesign the affairs of your life. From this point on you will begin to expand your use of these processes, focusing your attention upon conditions in the outer world as well as upon your immediate personal concerns.

You can apply these techniques to every situation in your life, for they are equally effective with nature, with animals and plants, with inanimate objects, as well as with organizations, groups and individuals. You have an unbelievable reservoir of power for potential good, power which you will eventually begin to recognize and acknowledge. The success of the programming in your daily life will be the most convincing of all proofs of the reality of this force.

Because many of us seem to have difficulty in believing in a process until we see that it actually works, we are giving you a few simple, foolproof exercises which will develop your proficiency in the techniques, and will simultaneously reinforce your beliefs in their effectiveness.

As these attempts succeed, your trust in your abilities will increase, and this will in turn enhance the power of your programming. Your growing confidence will give you the assurance to undertake increasingly ambitious projects.

One of the first ventures you might commence is the restructuring of an activity which is frustrating for many people: driving in traffic. Driving is a wonderful testing ground for your new skills, because you have many opportunities for practice, and because this is one activity in which you can quickly see the results of your efforts. Here are a few suggested experiments; you will be able to think of many more:

Exercise — Creating Parking Places

1. Relax and enter your meditative level.
2. Think of a time during the day when you will need a parking place.
3. Visualize yourself in your car on your visual screen.
4. See yourself driving smoothly into a parking place in the exact location you desire.
5. Repeat the process for each parking space you will need.
6. Release the scene from your visual screen.
7. Turn the results over to your Higher Self.
8. Come back to the outer level, clear your mind of the problem, and trust that all will be well.

* * * * * * * * * * * * * * * * * * * *

When you are ready, the desired parking places will await you just as you planned. Be diligent about following these steps, and soon an interesting phenomenon will occur. Your cooperative lower self, which knows all your needs, will take the initiative, and with no further instructions will quietly and efficiently provide spaces wherever and whenever required. You have established a new habit which resolves an irksome task with effortless ease.

The next exercise may seem to be beyond the scope of feasibility until you try it and prove to yourself its validity.

Exercise — Programming Green Traffic Lights

1. Relax and enter your meditative level.
2. See yourself in your car on your visual screen.

3. Visualize yourself moving easily and freely along the route you wish to travel.
4. See each traffic light you encounter turning green as you approach, so that your progress is smooth and uninterrupted.
5. Release the image from your inner screen.
6. Turn the results over to your Higher Self.
7. Return to the outer level, in full knowledge that all is being processed on another dimension.

* * * * * * * * * * * * * * * * * * * *

Again, continued practise with this exercise will create for your Lesser Self a new habit to facilitate your travel in traffic. Green lights will automatically precede you and traffic will adapt to insure your tranquil, even progress.

With the same method, you can eliminate bottlenecks whenever slow drivers are blocking the passing lanes.

Exercise — Dissolving Highway Bottlenecks

1. Do this exercise with your eyes open, while you are driving on the highway.
2. When you come to a driver whose slow pace in the passing lane impedes the speed of those behind him, drop into a meditative level. Keep your eyes open!
3. Send a telepathic message to the slow driver, mentally asking him to move aside. Be polite but firm.
4. Imagine the driver responding with the proper lane-change.
5. Release the image and any further thoughts about the situation.
6. Turn the results over to your Higher Self.
7. Direct your attention to another subject, so that your request can be projected into the Universe, where it will be acted upon as you requested.

* * * * * * * * * * * * * * * * * * * *

When commencing a trip, mentally program a successful, enjoyable journey:

Exercise — Planning a Journey

1. Before starting a trip, take a few moments to relax and enter your meditative level.
2. See yourself on your visual screen, embarking upon your journey.
3. Visualize yourself completely prepared, rested, with all your affairs in order. You are carefree and enthusiastic.
4. Program perfect weather, ideal travelling conditions, your vehicle functioning smoothly and efficiently.
5. See all the people you encounter being friendly, gracious, helpful.
6. Imagine yourself happy, enjoying the whole experience.
7. Program propitious timing, pleasant accommodations, delicious food, your expenditures as being less than expected.
8. Include some unforeseen benefits, some added spice and adventure.
9. See yourself arriving at your destination at the time you had selected, relaxed and refreshed, with the memory of a most satisfactory interlude in your life.

* *

The methods you apply to traffic can be adapted to other situations. Follow the same procedure: decide upon what you want, present it to your inner mind in specific detail, then release it to a Higher Power for implementation.

These exercises, which may seem elementary, are nonetheless valuable building blocks for more substantial undertakings. As stated before, success in small matters engenders confidence, which in turn feeds the fires of greater success. As you satisfy your skeptical, doubting, rational mind, you are preparing the way for your infinitely creative inner mind to function unimpeded.

Learning New Skills

One particularly rewarding application is in the development and enhancement of skills. You literally have the means now to learn anything you wish to learn, to acquire competence almost instantly, to attain exceptional expertise and mastery with an unbelievably small investment of time and effort. You have a wonderfully powerful ally, your Lesser Self, the ruler of the domain in which you will be operating.

You can become proficient in sports, for example, with singular ease using these techniques. Professional athletes, who have unlimited opportunities to test the effectiveness of the methods, have discovered this well-kept secret of the experts, and in ever-increasing numbers are utilizing these mental aids to polish their own performances.

To develop or improve an ability, spend time first in research to be sure that you understand proper form, the ideal standards you wish to emulate.

Exercise — Developing a Skill

1. Relax and enter your meditative level.
2. Project an image of yourself on to your inner visual screen.
3. See yourself performing the desired accomplishment with consummate skill and adeptship, enjoying your performance.
4. Take time to enact mentally all of the steps and processes which are involved in the actual activity.
5. Use all of your inner senses to experience the event fully and vividly; notice minute responses in your muscles and nerves.
6. Rejoice in the complete assurance with which you perform, the responsiveness of your muscles, the fine attunement of your body and mind which normally is

attained only through arduous, lengthy training.
7. Stay with the imaging as long as is comfortable, for you are establishing new neural pathways in your brain, while you instruct the mind in masterly accomplishment.
8. Release the scene from your visual screen.
9. Turn the results over to your Higher Self.
10. Now open your eyes and immediately reenact physically the exercise you have been processing mentally.

* *

You will be surprised at your excellent performance. Use the same procedure whenever you practice the activity, and you will master the skill in a remarkably short time, with outstanding expertise and pleasurable ease.

This ingenious method of learning has limitless possibilities: apply it not only to sports and physical activities of all kinds, but also to music, drama, sewing, accounting, public speaking. . . . . the list of potential skills you may acquire is boundless. You have the priceless opportunity to actually become a Renaissance man or woman, adept in every field of endeavor! What a veritable gift from the gods!

Results

Apply your programming arts to every facet of existence. Visualize yourself healthy, imagine harmonious interactions at home and at work, see yourself happy in all that you do. Be creative, focus your new talents upon every detail of your world, until you are satisfied with its perfection.

As each new challenge is met and surmounted, you will recognize that the experiences in which you triumph are but the surface indications of a deeper transformation. You will feel more and more that you are touching an inner well-spring of enormous power, a center of omnipresent good, which enables you to direct the course of your own destiny. You will become aware of gradual changes in your deepest attitudes about yourself, a sure and growing intimation of who you really are.

With this growing awareness, your personality will seem to soften, stresses will diminish, cares and trepidations recede. A marvelous sense of peace and serenity will underlie your actions; you will know beyond question that you are protected and sustained, that you are a unique and crucial element in the total design of life. Your bearing will express a radiant sweetness and nobility as you begin to exemplify the character of your own true self.

CHAPTER 11
REPROGRAMMING HABITS

One of the most challenging steps on the road to Self Mastery is the essential and rewarding project of evaluating and improving your habits and attitudes. Habits and attitudes are the province of the Lower Self, which accepts the directives you give (consciously or unconsciously) from your Middle Self, then effectively and unobtrusively carries out your mandates.

The Lesser Self has a limitless fund of power which it utilizes to support and insure optimum functioning during your earthly existence. Throughout your entire life, the Lesser Self has been efficiently performing its vital duties, sifting from volumes of material presented to it those which it deems essential.

The habits indoctrinated during childhood are deeply imprinted and resistant to change. These are the habits which assure adaptation to your individual environment, providing through wonderfully intricate and endless variations, a flexible pattern for existence. Because these habits are involved with actual survival, it is logical that they be solidly ingrained.

The Lesser Self uses its great power to create a stable base for the entire organism, relieving the Middle Self or Conscious Mind of the necessity for directing attention to repetitive details of living. Yet this Lower Self is acutely receptive to guidance and suggestion from the Conscious Mind.

As we have discussed, the Lesser Self is contacted or instructed through your thoughts, retaining as major programming those ideas upon which you dwell repeatedly or with particular emphasis. When you are able to communicate at will with the Lower Self in the deeper creative levels, you no longer need rely upon tedious repetition — you are now able to make impressions directly upon the inner mind. At this deeper level, it will accept suggestions readily, becoming a willing partner as you reprogram for change.

When you use this direct method to clear yourself of undesirable habits and restrictive attitudes, you are reforming your very nature, eliminating the major obstacles to inner growth.

We mentioned earlier that many of your problems originated in childhood. As a growing child you spent most of your formative years in the receptive and transformational levels of consciousness, forming the basic attitudes and habits which enable you to function in the world. You accepted as models your parents and those in your immediate environment, fashioning yourself trustingly and indiscriminately in their mold.

Studies show that by the time a child is four years old he has acquired half his basic attitudes and habits; by eight he has learned another thirty percent; by the age of fourteen he has acquired ninety percent of the attitudes and habits he will continue to use for the rest of his life. Most of these have been acquired without logic or reasoning, since these attributes develop with the maturing process.

Unfortunately, many of the characteristics handed down in this manner are negative in nature. Most of us are struggling to overcome the effects of experiences and habits acquired in childhood.

Such changes can be made easily and quickly by returning to the intuitive, creative levels where the habits and attitudes were originally impressed. We simply "reprogram", then replace old habits with new.

Steps in Reprogramming

You will be working from both outer and inner planes in reprogramming your habits, using three basic steps:
1. The first step is to make a decision to change.
2. The second step is to analyze the conditions contributing to the problem.
3. The third step is to utilize all of your inner and outer resources to resolve the issue.

You may feel that the first step is superfluous, for you have probably already decided to change the habit; in fact, you have been planning to do so for a long time. With reflection, however, you no doubt realize that you never made an absolute decision to eliminate the habit, nor set a specific time to start.

Your inner mind is fully aware that you have not yet made a concrete decision; it knows that you are still equivocating and postponing. So the first step is to pause, commit yourself, and know that you are ready for change.

You may be challenged by the inner self, which demands assurance that you really intend to disrupt your established pattern. At first you will feel strong compulsions to continue with your old ways, and may even discover to your dismay that fate is conspiring to dissuade you from such radical steps.

You may be presented with special inducements and unusual enticements which tempt you to continue the habit; a minor crisis may occur, and you decide to wait until the crisis abates before commiting yourself to your new undertaking. Your inner self will applaud your wisdom, reassured that you actually had no intention of changing.

However, if you are firm in your conviction and allow nothing to interfere with your progress, your inner self will realize that you are truly resolved to alter this habit. Suddenly you find that everything is easy, you no longer are tempted, and the pattern has been broken.

The inner self, as always, is eager to cooperate, to follow your bidding whenever that bidding is clear. Once the old pattern is disrupted, you can replace it with a constructive new pattern. You are fully capable of redesigning yourself in any manner you desire. . . . you are totally in charge of your world and all that transpires within it.

You Designed This Lifetime

Yet isn't this a contradiction? We have just discussed the impact of childhood programming by others in creating our attitudes, our habits, our very personalities. How can we be responsible for events which took place when we were impressionable children? The answer, again, comes from the inner planes.

One of the interesting exercises developed in many approaches to psychology and parapsychology is age-regression. Using various techniques, a person is able to remember and relive past experiences vividly and clearly, with complete recall of every fact. We discover with amazement the comprehensive quality of memory, where nothing is lost, all is stored, including the most inconsequential detail.

With therapists guiding them, people relive events of their childhood, re-experience birth or the prenatal period; some even find themselves in previous lifetimes, intimately involved in the adventures and concerns of another age.

Many subjects are able to attune themselves to higher levels of being, and to experience the interval before conception and birth. They see themselves surrounded by celestial beings, choosing the time and locale of birth, determining the nature of problems and opportunities they will encounter, selecting their parents.

If you were to go through this same awesome, exultant experience, you would no doubt share their common conviction: you would know with certainty that each of us personally designed the course of his own lifetime upon the earth, and that each is solely responsible for the nature of that course.

Thus you yourself chose the circumstances of your life, including your childhood programming and its resultant opportunities for growth. You are the architect of your destiny, not a victim of fate controlled by circumstances and manipulated by others. Recognize that you are in command of your world . . . you have created it, are constantly creating it anew with your thoughts and emotions; and you may deliberately decide to fashion a whole new creation.

Therefore, as you make a definite decision to alter an attitude or habit, know without question that you have complete power to do so.

Process for Change

If you have attempted to change a recalcitrant habit in the usual manner, you have undoubtedly studied and examined it extensively with your logical mind. You are aware of the background, the beginnings, the problems it creates.

It is time now to explore this habit from the inner dimensions, to see it from a different perspective, and to discover perhaps underlying aspects which may not be readily available to the outer senses.

Exercise — Reprogramming a Habit

1. Enter your workshop using the technique you learned in an earlier chapter.
2. Select a habit you wish to restructure.
3. Visualize your inner visual screen surrounded by a black frame.
4. On to the black-framed screen project images portraying all of the characteristics of the habit, exaggerating, visualizing symbolically if you wish.
5. See pictures of yourself indulging in the habit, with all of its consequences and side-effects.

6. If your habit involves money, imagine a great stack of coins, illustrating the amount of money you spend on that habit in one year. Repeat the stacks for previous years.

7. Look down upon the habit from a distance, observing the patterns of indulgence, the stimulations and inertia, the sense of invulnerability which has prevented change in the past. See the circumstances and thoughts which trigger indulgence.

8. Visualize yourself bound, or trapped by the habit.

9. Recognize that you have relinquished control of yourself to an outside force, that you have given that force a power it does not possess. You have been playing a game, and are now ready to end that game.

10. The black frame is an indication to your inner mind that you are exploring a problem, not creating, so list every facet of the problem you can recall.

11. When you feel that you have examined the habit in depth, imagine a big black "X" crossing out each image, write a big red "No" across the image.

12. Erase the scene from your screen, release it and let it go.

13. Tell yourself that never again, for the rest of your life, will you have the desire to indulge in this habit.

14. Visualize the bonds severed, the trap opened. Take a deep breath and feel yourself completely free.

15. Change the frame around your screen to sparkling white.

16. On to the white-framed screen project images portraying all of the benefits you will gain from changing the habit. You may visualize symbolically if you wish.

17. See the foe vanquished and yourself once more in command.

18. Visualize yourself on the screen, enjoying all of the advantages of your new habit patterns. Be aware of the emotions you feel; revel in the sense of accomplishment and well-being, the heady feeling of freedom which is

yours now that you are free from the habit. Experience
the scene fully.
19. With vivid images, visualize the new opportunities
   available with your new freedom.
20. Now on the mental calendar in your workshop, encircle
   a date a reasonable time in the future, and tell yourself
   that on that date you will have eliminated the habit, and
   will never again indulge in that habit.
21. Repeat this visualization several times daily, with the
   sure knowledge that on that day you will awaken
   released and free.
22. Revisualize the scenes on your white-framed screen
   frequently. This will reinforce your programming.

          *

   This is very effective, basic technique, to be used with
habits of all kinds.

Food and Eating Habits

   Some habits are harmful, seemingly with great power to
enslave. Our eating habits fall into this category, with most
of us hoping to alter our eating patterns in one manner or
another. One of the most common problems in our western
world is overweight; this is closely followed by cravings for
food which we know to be harmful to our bodies.
   Food is closely connected with memories and feelings
from our childhood, tied in with comfort, rewards, "growing
to be big and strong". Because they symbolize nurturing,
love and home, our eating habits are deep and basic. Yet we
are able to change even these powerful habits easily and
quickly from the inner plane, especially when we work also
with tools available on the outer plane.
   One of the most effective methods on the outer plane is to
refrain from eating for a short time, to fast. A brief juice

fast, for example, will disrupt established eating patterns. As the inner self relinquishes that programming, more desirable patterns may be reinstituted, incorporating proper quantity and types of food in addition to better scheduling. Inner programming will enable you to continue with the new pattern. While not essential, fasting can be most helpful.

Exercise — Changing Your Eating Habits

1. Enter your workshop level with the methods you have learned.
2. Visualize your inner screen surrounded by a black frame.
3. Now project onto your black-framed screen images of yourself with your patterns of eating.
4. Study those patterns, noting any you would like to change. Explore the emotions which may be indirectly responsible for these patterns.
5. Now project on to your black-framed screen images showing any individual foods which you feel might be causing a problem. Take your time while you review the foods you customarily eat.
6. When you feel that you have studied the situation thoroughly, you are ready for the next step: Mentally mark a big black "X", then write a big red "No" across the images of each undesired eating habit, over each item of food you consider a problem.
7. Now erase all of the images. . . . release them and let them go.
8. Mentally tell yourself that you will never again practice those eating habits, never again will you eat or have the desire to eat those particular foods.
9. Change the frame of your inner visual screen to white.
10. Project on to your screen images portraying your optimum patterns of eating, and see yourself happy with those new habits.
11. Project on to your screen images of food which is

healthful and nourishing; visualize yourself eating that food with enjoyment and pleasure, thoroughly happy and delighted with your new diet.

12. Picture yourself completing a wholesome meal, leaving extra food on your plate with a clear conscience; content and replete from the main portion of the meal, you have no desire for dessert.

13. Program that from now on, you will desire, eat and enjoy only those foods which are wholesome and nourishing, and in the quantities right for your body.

* * * * * * * * * * * * * * * * * * * *

This is a good exercise to redo periodically, as a way of reviewing the current status of your dietary patterns and evaluating the need for change. Most people have excellent response to the suggestions, and are able to remodel their eating habits easily. You will find your own rhythm. . . . perhaps you may need to repeat the exercise a number of times at first, until your inner mind adapts to the new regime.

Changing Weight and Proportions

The following exercise is remarkably effective in helping to reapportion your body's weight or measurements. You may modify the instructions for specific requirements, such as for gaining weight or for redistributing it in a special manner. The technique is successful by itself, but again we remind you to use outer aids as well as inner programming for balanced and long-lasting results.

Exercise — Altering Body Weight and Proportion

1. Whenever you wish to alter your weight or body proportions, take a few minutes before each meal to relax and enter your workshop level of awareness.

2. If you wish to lose weight, project onto your inner visual screen a scene showing all of the *excess* calories removed from your food and stacked along the edge of your plate. Picture the calories any way your imagination chooses, perhaps as tiny white marbles.
3. Then program your inner mind that your body will extract from the food you will be eating, all of the nourishment it needs for perfect health, and will discard the excess in a normal, natural, healthy manner.
4. Program that from now on, whenever you feel the desire to eat extra food between meals, all you need to do to eliminate that desire is to take three deep breaths and tell yourself that your appetite is satisfied. The desire to eat will vanish.
5. Encircle a date on your workshop calendar, a reasonable time in the future, and program that on that date you will have ideal weight and proportion.
6. Repeat the calendar visualization daily to reinforce the programming, and know that on the selected date the desired results will occur.
7. On your white-framed screen, visualize yourself with your desired weight and proportion. See yourself dressed in becoming clothes in the size and design you wish. Feel the new sense of ease you enjoy, knowing that your body is attractive.
8. Whenever thoughts of weight enter your mind, pause for a moment and picture yourself on your white-framed screen, exactly as you wish to be; your inner mind will manifest that vision.

* * * * * * * * * * * * * * * * * * * *

We remind ourselves again to use all tools available, both inwardly and outwardly, to achieve our goals. For example, recall again the great creative power of your words, and have your words work with you rather than against you. Examine your casual remarks to see if any of them may have been contributing to your problem, then rephrase them so they will add energy to the solution. Use only words and phrases which support your programming, positive expressions which attract positive experiences into your life.

As you apply these techniques, you will find that habits generally believed to be unalterable are actually fragile, and will respond readily to the command of your will.

In the next chapter you will put these processes to a more stringent test, and with the help of these and additional procedures will learn how you can overcome the most intractable of all habits, those known as "addictions".

CHAPTER 12
RELEASING ADDICTIONS

Some habits can exert such strong influence over us that we feel ourselves helpless, unable to discontinue or modify them even when we realize that such behavior patterns are destructive, that they can threaten health and relationships or even imperil our lives. Such powerful negative habits are called addictions.

As we examine ourselves with critical eyes, we discover that each of us has his own addictions uniquely tailored to his own individual vulnerabilities. For addictions are part of the adventure of growing, the great tempters, which test our commitment and determination to rise.

Yet few of us are aware that harmful thought patterns and substances can possess us and leave their marks upon our bodies and minds. We are altered unmistakably and predictably when we nurture our indulgences.

Usually a great deal of emotional energy is tied up in addictions; we often rationalize, or refuse to admit involvement. We may delude ourselves into thinking that destructive habits are acceptable because:

    a. Others are doing it.

    b. Our personal habit is less harmful than others.

    c. We like or enjoy it.

    d. We immaturely defend our rights to enslave ourselves, rejecting advice from caring friends.

    e. We fear isolation from contemporaries if we challenge popular customs.

Yet this dilemma is one of the steps on the path to

unfoldment. We must eventually garner the courage to stand up for our convictions and to turn our backs on the rule of the pack.

Of special importance are emotional habits and attitudes, for our lower emotions buttress the fortress of the Lesser Self. This is the arena in which most of us will meet our strongest challenges, as we learn to overcome our deeply ingrained negative feelings, prejudices, and attitudes toward life.

Yet these habits are just as responsive to transformation and change as are those issues which are more easily recognized. The magnitude of the habits and addictions you face is a measure of the strength you will gain when you overpower them.

Until you have faced an issue, realized its essence and overcome it, it will pursue you and recur — over and over. Yet once you have mastered a problem, you will never again encounter another one of that exact nature.

Your challenges will become very subtle as you grow in consciousness, as you meet and surmount the more obvious obstacles. Because of that subtlety and refinement, you may for a time not even recognize your problems. Considerable inner research may be required to identify the underlying causes of your difficulties, the basic issues you are to resolve.

As we turn our attention to types of addictions, the list of possibilities is endless. We will consider only a few of the most prevalent, and those which have special impact on the inner planes.

Food and Addictions

Different kinds of food fall into the category of addictions:
a. *Sugar*: one of the most widespread is the addiction to sugar, which is present in most of the processed food we eat. Many of us became addicted in infancy, through formulas, baby food, even sweetened water. White

sugar is a highly refined crystal which does not occur naturally in foods, thus our bodies have never developed a way of processing it.

From an esoteric standpoint, sugar is the essence of negativity in foods, carrying an intense negative energy, just as Vitamin E represents the opposite pole, embodying the highest spiritual essence of food.

b. *Coffee*: coffee is another widespread addiction. Although medical advisors have long advised patients to eliminate coffee, most of us have no realization of the profound effects it can have on our bodies. Popularly considered a pleasant, slightly "naughty" beverage, coffee's damages are actually severe, ranging from heart aggravation to interference with normal insulin production. Even a small amount can cause grave injury. Unfortunately, coffee, laden with chemicals, is the underlying cause of many of our most serious illnesses. On the inner planes, coffee dissolves a special golden protective essence which coats the nerves, resulting in symptoms of "nervousness" and interfering with the proper functioning of the nervous system. A comparable effect would be stripping insulation from electrical wires.

c. *Chocolate*: some people consider themselves "chocolaholics", possessed by an overwhelming craving for chocolate, one of our most highly addictive types of food. It contains the stimulants caffein and theobromine, as well as arsenic, and is a major cause of allergies.

Chocolate has a special quality which other types of food do not possess. It contains phenolethylamine, a substance (produced otherwise only by the pineal and pituitary glands) which creates in those who ingest it a euphoric feeling of well-being. This is the underlying reason for the traditional gift of chocolates to those we love, for its consumption envelops those who eat it in a warm and wonderful sensation of being loved.

Yet on the inner dimensions, chocolate is second only to refined sugar in its negative effects.

d. *Milk*: research shows increasing evidence that milk, nature's marvelous food for infants, can be harmful if ingested once a child is weaned, and that the milk of each species is the perfect food only for the babies of that species. Some scientists consider milk a primary cause of allergies, colds, ear and throat problems, and emotional disturbances. Others feel it is a major contributing factor in the development of many baffling and seemingly incurable illnesses.

Experiments have shown abnormally high levels of milk consumption among juvenile and adult prison inmates. Removal of milk from their diets has generally resulted in surprising reversals of antisocial feelings and behavior.

Milk and milk products, including cheese, ice cream and yoghurt, can be unexpectedly and powerfully addictive, and those affected are unusually resistant to change. For milk is closely associated with mother, home, nurturing, and to childhood reward and praise. Lifelong programming has persuaded most of us that milk is essential for good health.

Other Food Addictions

People can be addicted to black tea (which physically causes problems with the urinary tract), to salt, to refined foods and those with empty calories and little nourishment. In our modern larder, we have many opportunities for addiction, for as the body is overwhelmed with unbalanced and unnatural foods, it loses its innate ability to govern its appetites. When it is in a state of chemical imbalance, the body craves that with which it is saturated, seeks satisfaction with the toxin which is causing the imbalance . . . and addiction is the inevitable outcome.

Some addictions are subtle, less apparent than are those which manifest as cravings for various substances. People develop addictions to television, to football pools or mystery stories, to any pattern or habit which interferes with the optimum use of their time and thoughts, and which carries with it a feeling of compulsion.

Smoking, Alcohol and Drugs

When most people think of addictions, however, the usual reaction is to think immediately of smoking, alcohol and drugs, all of which can create serious problems. Researchers warn us repeatedly of the harm such toxins inflict upon our minds and bodies, while the results of the misuse of these toxins are widely observable in the lives of those around us.

Yet the most serious effects of these harmful substances are not readily apparent. Only those who have developed their higher powers of discernment can sense the true extent of the damage caused by these widespread habits; damage which is more destructive and far-reaching than the average observer can even imagine. As your sensitivity increases, you also will be able to perceive personally the injurious effects of these powerful poisons upon the finer bodies, the energy fields and the higher faculties of those who use them.

Because these addictions have such profound impact upon the inner being, and because they represent to many people some of life's greatest, most crippling problems, we will use them to demonstrate the procedures for nullifying the influence and power of addictive habits.

We will explore first the issue of smoking, presenting techniques which can be applied with equal effectiveness to alcohol and drugs, or to any other habit you wish to change.

Smoking

In addition to causing serious physical damage (which is well documented and widely publicized), smoking also presents other special problems to those who are seeking spiritual growth.

Tobacco not only lowers the vibratory rate of a smoker, it

also depresses the consciousness of anyone else in the room who is breathing the smoke. People who attempt to meditate in a smoke-filled room experience difficulty in reaching higher states of awareness, finding that they are unable to lift their awareness above the lower psychic dimensions, the astral levels of emotion and thought forms. Healers feel the same limitations.

Nature protects us by prohibiting our exposure to frequencies of vibration or consciousness beyond the maximum range we are capable of handling. Anything which creates toxins in our bodies lowers their vibratory rates, effectively preventing us from achieving higher states of awareness. We limit ourselves severely with our indulgencies and our appetites.

Thus we understand more deeply the repeated injunction common to spiritual teachers of all disciplines: the emphasis upon the need to purify all levels of being. . . . to purify our thoughts, our emotions, our bodies, our activities, our relationships, our surroundings. When we follow that injunction, and concentrate upon clearing out the contaminants in various aspects of our lives, the rewards are beyond imagining. . . . the immediate expansion of consciousness, the great inpouring of cosmic gifts is overwhelming.

In another sense, smoking has an even greater significance: those who study the science of consciousness place primary importance upon breathing and the breath. With each breath, we are breathing in life itself, special vital energy which not only sustains us but determines the quality of our being. A whole discipline of study revolves around various methods of controlling and directing the breath, with consequent changes in consciousness.

When we coat our lungs with impurities, we strike at the very essence of life itself, not only restricting the absorption of chemical elements necessary for the maintenance of our bodies, but preventing the assimilation of our full quota of vital life energy.

This deprivation is reflected in our emotions, our mental capacities, our interests and goals, in physical distress. . . . but most sadly apparent to those who see inwardly is the restriction of consciousness. We are limiting the breadth and reach of our very beings, settling for a half-life instead of the glorious potential which is our birthright.

With increased research, most of us realize that all members of a group are smoking when one member smokes, and we are becoming ardently protective of the purity of the air we breathe. This is not just a mental decision, but a reaction to real discomfort caused by our enhanced sensitivity to toxins. As we purify our bodies and raise our levels of awareness, we cannot tolerate impurities we formerly took in stride.

When we deal with an addiction, we are undertaking a project of completely different magnitude than the average habit. We are encountering a force with a spirit of its own. The spirit of tobacco can attach itself to us with relentless demand and control, a spirit with the added support of industry and social custom to magnify its power.

What methods do we use to overcome a habit which many have found extremely resistant to change? Because of the nature of the habit, we can understand the wisdom of working with all methods available, both inwardly and outwardly.

Of greatest importance is a firm decision to stop smoking. Sometimes smokers resist the urgings of others who want them to stop, feeling the need to assert their own independence by refusing to change. As they review the whole impact of smoking upon their lives, however, they realize the inappropriateness of this attitude.

The first step is to make an unequivocal decision to stop, and to stop immediately.

Exercise for Overcoming Addictions: Smoking

1. Enter your meditative level with your usual method. Envision yourself on your black-framed screen.

2. Review your whole history of smoking. See yourself beginning to smoke.
3. Recapture the tastes and sensations of your first experience.
4. Ask yourself your reasons for starting:
    a. Did you start in your teens, as a sign of rebellion against parental authority?
    b. Were you seeking popularity, the acceptance of your peers?
    c. Did you wish to appear older, more sophisticated?
5. Explore your own reasons for commencing the habit, then ask yourself the question, "How many of these reasons apply now?" Perhaps you have outgrown your basic reasons for smoking.
6. Examine your history in perspective. See the patterns of habit, the events which have been influenced by your smoking, the forfeiture of time and energy it requires.
7. Determine the amount of money you spend in a year, visualizing a stack of coins or bills.
8. Now see yourself spending that money instead on something you would dearly like to have. When you stop smoking, you may actually reclaim that amount to spend as you wish.
9. On the black-framed screen, project the pattern of one of your days, noticing all of the occasions when you normally smoke.
10. In your role as observer, imagine a huge eraser in your hand. Now reach out and from each scene, erase the image of the cigarette in your hand.
11. See yourself retaining the full sense of happiness you are experiencing in each scene, so engrossed in your activity you don't even miss the cigarette.
12. Now on your black-framed screen, picture all of the negative qualities about smoking you can recall. Dramatize them, exaggerate them, symbolize them.
13. Visualize the effects upon different areas of your body: imagine your impaired senses of taste and smell, the accelerated aging process, the coarseness of your skin

and hair, the roughness of your voice, the impairment of every body system.

14. Intensify the acrid tobacco stench in your home, your clothes, your car.

15. Picture yourself in various graphic poses:
    a. Enshrouded in a black cloud of smoke, coughing and wheezing.
    b. Sputtering along in low gear on your highway of life.
    c. Bowed over carrying an enormous black burden upon your back.
    d. Give your imagination free rein as you picture every detail of every scene you imagine.

16. When you feel that you have visualized all of the negative qualities, cross out each image with a big black "X" and write across it a big red "NO".

17. Now erase all of the images, release them and let them go, telling yourself you will never again have the slightest desire to smoke.

18. Change the frame's color to white, and project onto the screen images of yourself completely free from the habit.
    a. For example, visualize yourself running joyously in the sunshine, breathing deeply and fully the crystalline clear air; sense a wonderful cleanliness and freshness surrounding you, a lightness and responsiveness to your body.
    b. See all of your body systems functioning smoothly and perfectly; experience an exuberant overabundance of energy.
    c. Imagine yourself suddenly unshackled, with the bonds lying severed on the ground.
    d. Relish your highly enhanced senses, savour fragrances and flavors you have not experienced for years.
    e. Imagine the feeling of release, the true sensation of freedom you will experience, the victory in knowing that you have conquered a formidable foe.
    f. Visualize yourself enfolded in a feeling of peace and

well-being, serene and harmonious in a marvelous new attunement with nature and life.

19. Allow your imagination to expand freely, as you strengthen your visualization with expectancy and the knowledge that it will all take place.

20. Picture your mental calendar, encircling a date a reasonable time from today, and tell yourself that on that date you will stop smoking, and will never smoke nor have the desire to smoke again in your entire life. Repeat this visualization and affirmation several times daily, whenever you can. When you awaken on the morning of the designated day, you will be completely free from any compulsion to smoke.

21. Program a cue which will eliminate the urge to smoke. For example, program that three deep breaths or a drink of water will eliminate the desire to smoke.

22. Program that you will effect this change easily and effortlessly, with no undesirable side-effects.

* * * * * * * * * * * * * * * * * * *

There is no need to experience any adverse side-effects when you stop smoking. If you have been warned that you would inevitably gain unwanted weight at that time, disregard these forebodings as self-fulfilling prophecies. You will acquire extra weight only if you program yourself with the belief and expectation that you will.

Begin to categorize yourself as a non-smoker rather than as a smoker; mentally call yourself a non-smoker, sit in non-smoking sections of airplanes and restaurants, refer to the past as the time when you used to smoke. Use every aid available in a concentrated assault upon the habit.

Smoking — Nutrition

On the outer level, nutrition is of critical importance in combatting any addiction, but the benefits of therapeutic nutrition are probably most immediately noticeable during the change from smoking to non-smoking. Nutritional therapy can help nature cleanse the body of toxins, can subdue cravings by balancing body chemistry, can calm emotions and alleviate stress. With proper diet and correct supplements, you can transform the reformation from a struggle into a smooth, gentle transition.

A basic approach suggested by many nutritionists is as follows:

1. Eliminate all sugar and highly refined foods from your diet.
2. Help nature cleanse your system of poisons with increased amounts of Vitamin C, Vitamin E, and concentrated essence of garlic.
3. Use a dietary supplement rich in vitamins, minerals, and enzymes to help correct any nutritional deficiencies.
4. Reinforce this foundation with a stress formula supplement, which includes maximum amounts of amino acids and the B Vitamins, with added glutamic acid, Vitamin B15, niacin or niacinimide. Excellent results are also obtainable with herbs.

With this type of nutritional program, you will not only simplify the process of changing your habit, but as an added benefit will acquire a wonderful sense of exuberance and renewed vitality.

Although smoking may have seemed an insurmountable obstacle in the past, by using these extraordinarily effective methods a person can eliminate the habit rapidly, comfortably and permanently.

Alcohol

Alcohol is the cause of some confusion among those on the spiritual path, who see mounting destruction of lives caused by overindulgence, yet hear of beneficent effects when it is used as a remedy for illness. Wine, especially, has acquired a special mystique. Such seekers may value alcoholic beverages for their helpful qualities without taking into consideration their total impact.

Most people are unaware of the influence which even light drinking has upon them; they will be astonished to realize that the effects of one drink are readily apparent to a sensitive observer, who can see radical changes in the drinker's aura and feel immediate alterations in his energy field.

Alcohol is a toxin affecting the body and spirit in whatever form it is taken.

Most psychic and spiritual healers will not attempt to heal when they have indulged in alcohol, for they have learned that their powers are diminished and unpredictable. Experienced meditators will refuse to meditate after drinking alcoholic beverages, realizing that they will be attuned to lower, less desirable levels of awareness.

Many alcoholics today are highly evolved individuals whose fine sensitivity cannot handle the coarse vibrations of alcohol.

Fortunately, those on the spiritual path will usually find that their desires for alcohol gradually diminish, with no special decisions of their own. Their higher inner guidance is directing them gently toward purification and upliftment of their beings; eventually they will have no interest or enjoyment in alcohol, and will have uncomfortable reactions if they should indulge.

Once a person has experienced the clarity and pleasure which results from refinement of his higher senses, he is impatient and repelled when that clarity is impaired. He can hasten that refinement by making a deliberate decision to forego alcohol, rather than waiting for the slower processes of evolvement.

One serious hazard of alcohol and alcoholism is the possibility of opening oneself to the influences of the astral or emotional level of consciousness. Alcohol lowers the protective walls which shield us from those lesser levels of being, and can invite lower influences into our own energy fields. This subject is discussed in greater detail later in the chapter.

Drugs

Drugs are among our most potent addictions. Many of our pharmaceutical drugs are extremely powerful, causing deep concern to medical practitioners. Often drugs which at first were considered non-addictive have later proven to be acutely addictive. We have no way of foreseeing the far-reaching impact of our expanding pharmacy.

All of the addictions we are considering have harmful effects upon the whole of our beings, for as one part is damaged, so is the total. Some substances, however, seem to inflict most harm upon the physical body, others upon the mental or emotional. Alcohol and tobacco affect especially the feeling nature, with definite disturbances of the astral, emotional level. Psychedelic drugs by their very nature have profound effects upon the more sensitive higher intuitive bodies.

We have always had psychedelic drugs with us, in every culture. However, in the past these drugs have been regarded with deep respect and reverence, reserved exclusively for occasions of initiation and spiritual quest, and dispensed only through shamans or spiritual teachers. The drugs were employed merely to point the way. . . . a candidate was instructed after the initiation in techniques which would permit him to reach these same levels of consciousness safely and naturally without chemical assistance. These substances were never intended to be used indiscriminately, to be abused by wholesale, destructive over-indulgence.

These methods of initiation, moreover, belong to the last age. They are no longer necessary nor desirable, for mankind has progressed far beyond the scope of such aids. All drugs damage the finer bodies, thus setting their own limits of effectiveness.

Many of those who have sought enlightenment through drugs have subsequently abandoned that path, for they seemed to reach a barrier which prevented further expansion. There is a ceiling, a limit to the degree of consciousness which may be achieved in this manner. Progress beyond that ceiling demands a purity and clarity which is obscured and prevented by drugs.

Drugs — Marijuana

One drug is especially hazardous to those on the quest for higher consciousness; from a metaphysical viewpoint, it is probably the most dangerous substance on the planet. This drug is marijuana.

Marijuana, like other addictive substances, affects the whole organism, creating its own physical, emotional and mental problems. On the physical level, marijuana may reach far beyond the individual involved, for scientific investigations reveal that it may interfere with genetic reproduction and could weaken the inherited potentials of future generations.

On a mental level, marijuana again has its own distinctions, for it damages cells in the cerebral cortex (the most highly evolved part of our brains), destroying the ability to look ahead to the future, to set goals and make plans. Since the discriminating faculties of the brain are deadened, those addicted to marijuana maintain the staunch conviction that they are completely unaffected, yet the impartial observer can notice definite and serious adverse changes.

However, our deeper concern is the effect of marijuana upon the inner being. Marijuana disables the third eye (which mystics describe as a vortex of energy resembling a crystal) found in the center of the forehead, close to the pineal gland. This important vortex acts as a transformer, enabling us to evolve to higher states of consciousness. It is the doorway through which we will move into the consciousness of the incoming age. Marijuana destroys that capability.

If you are able to perceive auras, you can actually see how marijuana affects the third eye center. A grey cloud will appear in the energy field around the head, with a special dense concentration in the center of the forehead. The appearance is unmistakable and discouraging, as darkness localizes in this critically sensitive area which is rightfully a powerful vortex of clear light.

The cloud will linger for weeks or months after the drug's use is stopped; in some cases years may be required to restore the pineal center to optimal functioning. Even occasional use obscures the divine connection with higher awareness, and makes far more difficult the quest for self-mastery.

This addiction falls into a different category from other habits and addictions, and requires the assistance of specially trained individuals. When you make the decision to change, be firm and unyielding in that decision. Employ all of the techniques for habit control we have discussed, apply the nutritional aids mentioned, and use the white light exercise (which you will be learning soon) faithfully and frequently.

Then find a spiritual or psychic healer who will cleanse your aura and apply his special skills in repairing the serious damage to the sensitive inner bodies. If he is able to restore the pineal center to health, guard yourself carefully from injury, for it is important that you do not slip back into the habit. Some healers feel that they can bring this center back to proper functioning only once; after that the damage may be permanent.

Spirit Energy

Everything has energy, all things contain consciousness. Some addictive substances have a strong consciousness or spirit of their own. Alcohol and narcotics, for example, have their own spirits, as does sugar.

In addition, as we mentioned, the use of powerful negative substances can breach your protective auric shield, permitting the entrance and attachment of lower spirit forms or entities. These spirits and entities can actually create and increase one's appetite for an addictive substance, causing the illusion that one's appetite is no longer under control. Jesus spoke of spirits when he gave instructions to "heal the sick, raise the dead and cast out evil spirits."

People who have clairvoyant skills are able to see these spirits and entities. Graduating students in one parapsychology class were taken to a bar which was a favorite gathering place of advanced alcoholics (or winos) and told to sit quietly and observe with inner vision. When they left they were asked to describe what they had seen.

All of them were appalled to see over each alcoholic a shadowy form, seemingly attached to the back of his neck. This was the spirit entity or spirit of alcohol, urging that person to drink. Parapsychologists and psychic or spiritual healers are trained to remove these forces and to protect the subject from further attachment.

If you are correcting habits which may involve strong negative spirit energies, such as alcohol, smoking or drugs, follow the same potent procedures we suggested for marijuana addiction: use your white light exercise regularly and frequently, and enlist the aid of a skilled spiritual healer, who will be able to assist you in freeing yourself from these habits more rapidly and easily.

Emotional Reaction

As we discuss various habits, observe your emotional reaction. You may nod sagely as you agree that people really should eliminate those addictive habits which don't apply to you. When we mention one of your particular habits, however, your response suddenly changes. You are immediately alert, on the defensive. Your Lesser Self may feel its control challenged, and will summon all of its reserves to thwart the assault.

Listen to the excuses and rationalizations which flood your mind, the indignation you feel because your own private habit is being questioned. These are typical reactions:

1. You may tell yourself that this is your life and your body, and you have a right to conduct your life in any way you choose.

2. You may retort that since you refrain from indulgence in other damaging habits, you are entitled to one little vice.

3. You may counter with the popular rationalization that all things are acceptable in moderation.

4. You may respond with the amazing deduction, occasionally voiced by spiritual seekers, that smoking or sugar will ground your energies, carefully overlooking the other proven, effective methods which will ground you safely and healthfully.

5. However, your strongest vindication, you tell yourself, is the fact that you continue this habit only because you enjoy it, which of course is the only reason that any of us indulge in any of these habits.

6. You reassure yourself that you are not actually addicted; you are capable of quitting any time you wish, but there really is no reason to stop now.

All of these responses are logical, convincing excuses, which your Lesser Self sincerely believes. Appreciate its genius for protection, for maintaining continuity and order, but recognize that these thoughts emanating from your lower self represent a desperate bid to maintain the status-quo.

Do not delegate the precious power of making decisions to this part of your being. When you are firm in your commitment to change, your Lesser Self will adapt gracefully to new directions.

Once you are determined to free yourself from destructive

habits, an encouraging fact emerges: when you have discontinued the habits and cleared yourself of toxins, using the methods we have been discussing, within a period of time much of the damage resulting from these detrimental practices can be repaired.

The body and mind have remarkable powers to regenerate themselves. As we stimulate and direct these powers with our thoughts and with the techniques we have been learning, we discover that we can actually rejuvenate our bodies and renew our minds.

Turning to a Higher Power

As we have explored different effective methods for dealing with habits, we have suggested procedures that utilize techniques which function upon both outer and inner planes. It is important to apply all of these methods, important to examine, evaluate, and commit yourself unequivocally to change. By investing your time and energy, by studying the ramifications of the habits and their meaning in your life, you gain a richer, deeper understanding of yourself.

Now there is one final process which is more powerful than anything we have yet considered, one which draws upon resources of far greater magnitude than any you by yourself can muster. It is time to encompass the problems and all you have learned from them, then turn them over to Higher Consciousness . . . time to ask for help.

You do not have to do it all yourself! This acknowledgement may be the great underlying lesson you are to learn from your contest with a particular habit, especially one which seems to be an insurmountable addiction.

A major step on the journey which will free you from domination by your Lesser Self is to ask for help and guidance from your Higher Self. As you turn yourself over to Higher Guidance, with sincere requests for help, then release your worries and let them go, you will tap into an immense power, one which is always available and ready for you to use.

The following exercise is wonderfully freeing and joyous.

Exercise — Turning your Problem over to a Higher Power

1. Enter your meditative level with the methods you have learned.
2. On your mental screen, visualize your habit symbolically, with all of its multiple aspects and ramifications. See it as an image, a form.
3. Now create a giant bubble.
4. Place the image depicting your habit inside the bubble and seal it securely within.
5. Now watch the bubble begin to rise slowly, then more swiftly, higher and higher.
6. See it wafted away, up into the clear, sunny sky, until it finally disappears, absorbed in luminous, radiant light.
7. Feel yourself completely free from all worry or concern, for you have released your problem to a higher power, and all will be well.

* * * * * * * * * * * * * * * * * * * *

The Critical Urgency of Conquering Your Habits Now

You now have a brief overview of the important role habits and addictions play in your life. You have been practicing techniques for screening those habits, and have discovered your own powers to edit and control.

You can recognize the critical urgency of eradicating as quickly as possible any habits or addictions which oppress you or reduce the quality of your life.

Every negative habit is a major deterrent to future advancement, but is at the same time, a challenge and opportunity custom-designed specifically for you. The more apparently insurmountable the habit, the greater the potential for growth.

When you conquer a powerful habit, you exult in a jubilant sense of triumph and freedom. In gaining mastery over this aspect of yourself, you have attained a supreme victory.

Study each habit closely, for the problems you encounter when you are on this path are initiations. Upon reflection, each problem will reveal itself to be rich in symbology, paralleling those adventures recounted in legends, recorded by sages.

As you read the myths of legendary journeys and mystical encounters, you suddenly realize that you are reading about yourself. The great universal sagas reveal to you a deeper insight into the true nature and more profound meanings of your own experiences.

Thus it is impossible to overestimate the importance of conquering your habits. You are doing far more than overcoming inconvenient and annoying traits. In conquering your habits, you are molding your character, altering your personality, stimulating profound changes within your deepest being.

You are shifting the balance of power from enslavement by the Lesser Self to dominion by the Greater Self, moving from the excesses of childhood to the harmony and wisdom of maturity.

For habits are the domain of the Lower Self, useful, essential, powerful, but merely tools. Under the guidance of the Higher Self, these tools are the means for creating a perfect life. Thus, mastering your habits is an essential, critical undertaking, fraught with urgency, not a mere distasteful chore, to be postponed and extended indefinitely. Since habits are the major impediments obstructing your way, face them, concentrate upon them, and conquer them now. . . . you have all of the means and power you need.

The Blueprint of Your New Being

Whenever you work with habits, you are dipping briefly into the negative realm of problems, so that you may identify them, correct them and free yourself from their influence.

Once you have processed a habit or addiction, it is important to lift yourself out of that lower vibration and attune yourself to the higher frequency of your real being, that ideal image on the inner plane which is the model and blueprint upon which you are creating your new perfect self.

Exercise — The True You

1. If you were to glimpse momentarily the nature of your true being, you would realize that habits which seem overwhelming are actually transient and easily altered. We are about to take such a glimpse. . . .
2. Enter your meditative level, and place the white frame around your inner visual screen.
3. Project onto the screen an image of yourself with a perfect body: a body you envision to be magnificent in every way; ideal weight and proportion, excellent condition, a body beautiful, balanced and harmonious.
4. Now experience yourself in this wonderful body. Feel the strength and smoothness of your muscles, the lightness and grace of your movements, the regality of your bearing. Rejoice in the glorious sense of happiness and well-being which accompanies a perfectly functioning body.
5. Be aware of the harmony and balance uniting all levels of your being, a deep, all-pervading sense of peace and oneness with all life.
6. Feel your emotions uplifted. . . . you are forgiving, compassionate and understanding. You are serene and secure, filled with a deep love for yourself and for all of humanity.

7. Your thoughts are clear and keen, imbued with wisdom. Your mind is attuned to the Source of All Knowledge.
8. Know that you are actually experiencing the Real You. On higher dimensions, every part of your being is absolutely perfect. This perfect self is the blueprint and model toward which all of the creative forces within you are building.
9. Everything within you is striving for perfection; only your own thoughts and emotions can interfere with the manifestation of that perfection.
10. In the future, whenever you think of yourself, visualize that perfect being you are experiencing now, superb in every way, and know that this is an expression of the Real You.
11. Pause frequently during each day to attune to your Real Self. Experience the full glory and unlimited potential of your beautiful inner being, with the certainty that this ideal is gradually taking form as your true reality on the outer dimension as well as upon the inner.
12. With your thoughts you create; create now and manifest that perfect self which is your birthright.

* * * * * * * * * * * * * * * * * * *

CHAPTER 13
SURRENDER

W hat a heady experience it is to discover your own power to plumb and test the latent potency of your thoughts! As you read this book, you are first presented with theories, then given progressive exercises which demonstrate these theories, thus enabling you to prove their effectiveness for yourself. Through your own experiences you are transferring these concepts from the realms of beliefs and doubts into the realm of conviction.

This is a continuing process, converting the deeply ingrained prejudices and limited beliefs of a lifetime into a sound foundation composed of open receptivity and the secure knowledge of your own unlimited potential.

The next step in developing this foundation is to begin observing yourself from a different perspective. Most of us are so engrossed in living our lives that we fail to perceive life's lessons, or comprehend its meaning. So it is wise to establish a habit of withdrawing periodically, of becoming detached and impersonal, and examining your life from a distance. When you do, you will be able to discern patterns and trends, sets of similar circumstances which are repeated over and over until you finally learn the lessons they embody.

From this objective viewpoint you may catch an inkling of the all-encompassing wisdom guiding your footsteps. As patterns begin to emerge, you can perceive the underlying purposes in crises and traumatic events. You can appreciate the strength you gain and the changes in direction you choose because of trying experiences. With your broader understanding, you are able to make more capable decisions, to avoid many mistakes.

Life does not necessarily demand suffering as the inevitable price for learning its lessons. We are given an option:

1. We may master its curriculum the hard way, through dreary repetition of increasingly painful experiences, or
2. We may attain the same ends with relative ease, through vicarious experience and perspicacious observation.

Your own life is a fascinating study. Your newly expanded perspective will give you two valuable advantages: first, a ring-side seat to all of the action, and secondly, a wonderful new sense of trusting acceptance and divine purpose.

If you have been practicing the exercises in this book, you have by this time accumulated considerable proof of the phenomenal creative potency of your thoughts. As you step back now and observe yourself and others from a distance, you can see the beautiful impartiality and implacability of the laws of reciprocity and creativity.

From such observation and from your own unfolding adventures you are gradually convinced that every quality of your life. . . . your success or failure, your happiness or unhappiness, the warf and woof of your present existence and of your future. . . . is determined by your current thoughts and emotions, those you are experiencing right now. With a sense of high exhilaration, you realize that you actually can order your life to your own design, unique and totally fulfilling.

Yet paradoxically, as you move from impotence to the knowledge of omnipotence, you will soon discover that a still greater lesson is involved: you are learning to control your life, only to surrender that control.

Your normal awareness is centered in your Lesser Self. . . . in your conscious rational mind and your subconscious, lower emotional mind. Through these important components of your being you are focusing and manifesting great creative energy, which is fine and proper. However, the actual direction of your life is not the prerogative of your Lesser Self, even though it may seek to claim it. Your Higher Self, which knows your over-all purpose and reason for existence, is the architect of your destiny. The Low Self is the servant of the High Self, the unilluminated but remarkably capable instrument for accomplishing your mission upon the earth. Thus the control of your life must be relinquished by the child-like Lesser Self and entrusted to the wise, benevolent dominion of the Higher Self.

Free Will and Adversity

When you use your new skills to fulfill your desires, as you take the resolution of your problems into your own hands, you are invoking one of the great gifts of the earth plane, the gift of free will. You have been granted the precious privilege of fashioning your own life into the design of your choosing. You have the power to create a masterpiece. . . . or a caricature. The choice is entirely yours.

In the past, we all enjoyed great latitude, we were free to squander our resources and scatter our attention. We have been able to meander along inviting byways and sideroads on our paths to our goals. Now, however, in this time of crisis and cosmic upheaval, we no longer have that option. Each of us has his own work of crucial importance, special tasks that only he can perform.

Your work is of even greater import than that of most people, for you have stepped beyond the torpid evolution of the masses; you are embarked upon a mission which is divinely ordained. Timing is exquisitely critical. Any deviation now from your destined purpose will meet with swift reversals. If you do not voluntarily follow that straight route, your Higher Self will compel your cooperation.

Study the world around you with your new detached

perspective, and you will see this force in operation, in the lives of others as well as in your own.

In many cases, the even tenor of a person's existence erupts suddenly into a series of distressing events, one disaster following another. Nothing seems to stem the tide. Eventually he reaches a point of total despair, for he has exhausted his own capabilities. . . . he is immobilized by a crushing sense of failure.

In this hopeless situation, he finally admits defeat; he gives up. This surrender is felt deeply on every level of his being, in physical, mental, and emotional reactions. He recognizes his own fallibility, and knows he cannot continue further alone.

In desperation, as a last resort, he turns to a divine power greater than himself and asks for help. Amazingly, incredibly, his prayer is answered! His plea has halted the debacle, engendered a turning point, and miraculously everything changes. Conditions improve, solutions appear, attractive opportunities offer themselves. His spirits are lifted, his hopes reborn as he is presented with stimulating alternatives and new visions.

He has discovered and invoked a basic universal law: "Ask and it shall be given" (Matthew VII, 7-8); "Ask in prayer, believing, and ye shall receive" (Matthew XXI, 22). He has surrendered control of his life from the dominion of the limited Lesser Self to the dominion of the limitless Higher Self.

The process of surrender, of turning oneself over to higher guidance, is an essential phase of the spiritual journey, one which is emphasized in every religion and esoteric teaching. This is not merely an intellectual commitment. . . . it is an actual surrender, a relinquishment of authority which is accepted and acknowledged by the Lesser Self on all of its planes of being.

Usually, the first reaction is an almost instant sense of freedom, as if an intolerable burden has been lifted. This is followed by a deeply joyous certainty that all is well.

Thereafter, problems seem to resolve themselves through solutions unforeseen or unimagined, resulting in ultimate benefit for all concerned.

Catastrophies impress their lessons graphically and unmistakably; yet such havoc, as we said, is not mandatory for spiritual evolvement. If one is wise and receptive, if he evaluates and attempts to understand the meaning of his experiences, he is able to progress with much greater comfort through the stages of growth. He can surrender voluntarily to the beneficient sovereignty of the Higher Self, and thus avoid countless misfortune. The sole objective of such adversity is the subjugation of the Lesser Self to the leadership of the Higher Self, the divinity within.

This covenant must occur through one's own volition, for free will is just that, the freedom to choose for any moment the motivating force, the level of guidance which is to operate at that moment in one's life. Free will is truly a gift of God, a power we are learning to use to further our own evolvement.

Spirals of Growth

As we in our individual lives parallel the evolution of mankind, we move from the stages of childhood through adolescence into maturity. Advancement occurs by means of many overlapping, interweaving spirals of growth, any one of which may be frozen through trauma at levels of immaturity.

When we objectively observe ourselves and those around us, we note that each of us encompasses many different phases of growth within his own complex structure. In some ways we act as infants, in other ways as adults. As a composite of all these spirals, we each attain a balance, an over-all comprehensive degree of maturity.

During the developmental period of childhood, a person is under the domination of the Lesser Self; conversely, an adult will, ideally, have completed his union with his Higher

Self. Adolescence is the turbulent period of transition, spiritually as well as physically and emotionally, as the Lesser Self strives to retain its command while gradually succumbing to the growing ascendency of the Higher Self.

The majority of people, regardless of age, are still manifesting the general characteristics of childhood, governed by the emotions and urges of the Lower Self. Some have attained spiritual adolescence, and are deeply involved in the turmoil of transition, as they cope with the conflicting demands of two sides of their natures. Very few of us have reached full spiritual maturity, the state of self-realization or oneness with the divinity within us.

Because you have taken charge of your own progress, you may, with the assistance of your High Self, condense or avoid much of the agitation of adolescence. You are learning to release voluntarily the restraints of the Lesser Self and to advance consciously into the illustrious state of spiritual maturity.

The decision to turn yourself over to the guidance of your higher nature is not one which is made once and then forgotten. It must be repeated and repeated until the change is firmly anchored. For we are discussing one of the primary purposes of life itself, the process of transformation, the actual method for moving from lower consciousness into higher consciousness.

These states of being are worlds apart, yet there is a secret bridge, an avenue for progressing from one to another. The heart of this secret span is surrender.

Process of Surrender

Now that we have acknowledged the importance of surrender, how do we actually initiate the process? We will use a specific exercise, a simple step-by-step procedure, which like most of the others you have learned seems remarkably easy yet is potent and effective. This exercise is to be done daily immediately upon awakening.

Each day is in essence a new beginning, a miniature lifetime complete within itself. The nature of free will requires that a commitment be made, dedicating that day to the province of the High Self. The High Self will not by itself take command. It will assume that role only when it is offered voluntarily by the conscious mind.

When you go to sleep at night, you release your hold upon the affairs of your earthly existence, and ascend to far higher realms of consciousness. Upon awakening, you return again to pick up the strands of your earthly life, to adopt the karmic pattern of the day.

Each day has its lessons to impart, lessons determined in part by the laws of cause and effect. You are to reap the consequences of past thought and action, by garnering the rewards from your positive contributions, and by repaying and atoning for negative activities.

Each morning, however, you are given an opportunity to alter that pattern. For a brief time between waking and sleeping, the influences of the incoming day are nebulous as they have not yet crystallized. During those few moments, you may easily detach yourself from the laws of karma (cause and effect), which govern the earthly plane, and place yourself instead under the jurisprudence of the laws of grace, which function on the spiritual planes. You do this by asking for help, then turning dominion of the day over to higher guidance.

The whole tenor of the day shifts suddenly and dramatically. Your way becomes smooth and effortless, as everything seems to flow. Only those persons and events which are beneficial for you will enter your sphere this day. You no longer fret nor worry about the future, for you sense the presence of a loving intelligence which protects, directs, and inspires you. You feel contented and happy, facing your world with expectancy and anticipation. Miraculous changes will take place in your life, continuing evidence of the providence sustaining you.

Exercise — Surrendering Yourself to Higher Guidance

1. This exercise is to be done daily upon awakening.
2. As you gradually become aware of the first faint stirrings of returning consciousness, pause for a few moments, and gather your drowsy thoughts.
3. Observe yourself objectively, and acknowledge that from the viewpoint of your rational mind (your Lesser Self), you are limited and vulnerable. Admit to yourself that without divine guidance you are unable to cope wisely or proficiently with the unknown issues of the forthcoming day.
4. Now become aware of the loving presence of your nurturing, all-caring High Self, waiting patiently for your attention.
5. Sense the omnipotence, the vast wisdom, and above all the keen interest of this Higher Self, its total involvement in all your affairs.
6. Then with the trust of a child asking the support of a strong and devoted parent, mentally phrase a request such as this: "Please help me. I cannot handle this day alone. . . . I need your guidance and assistance. I turn myself over completely to you. Thank you."
7. You will be flooded instantly with an exquisite sensation of release and relief, with the warmly comforting knowledge that you have transferred authority to a benevolent power which will pilot you safely through the reefs and shoals of a new day.
8. Open your eyes and start your day with cheer and reassurance that that which is best for you awaits you.

* * * * * * * * * * * * * * * * * * *

Even though you have established a contract with your Higher Self, your own free will is always paramount, and at any time may withdraw from that agreement. You will probably have subtle opportunities during the day to either affirm or rescind that contract, to renew your commitment to higher guidance or transfer command to the Lesser Self.

Under the proper stimuli, the patterns of response which have governed your past behavior will tend to reassert themselves, for you are still in a state of transition, of solidifying your merger with your greater being. Minor upsets and disturbances will undoubtedly continue to arise to test your dedication. If you react from your new center of understanding, trusting higher intelligence to handle the problems, the situations will resolve themselves effortlessly and brilliantly.

If, on the other hand, you respond to the challenges intellectually or emotionally, drawing upon the resources of the. Lesser Self, you will probably find the situations disintegrating swiftly into insolvable impasses. On your new level of evolvement, these less potent capabilities no longer suffice.

Though previously you may have been able to extricate yourself from predicaments through your wits, now you are rapidly immobilized on all fronts, until you remember to call upon your powerful ally. This must be done consciously and deliberately, a voluntary surrender and petition for help.

Be sure to release completely any worries or fear of the outcome, for worry and fear will cause discordant energy to coalesce in your magnetic field, thus postponing the solution.

Invoking Higher Guidance During the Day

The technique you will probably find most convenient to use during the day is the bubble visualization you employed when you were reprogramming habits.

Exercise:

1. Visualize your situation or problem symbolically, perhaps imagining yourself in a cloud of unknowing.

2. Mentally create an immense bubble, and place your envisioned problem inside. Include all worries or concerns about the problem.
3. Mentally ask for help, admitting that your logical mind is incapable of knowing all of the answers, and you therefore surrender dominion of yourself to a higher divinity.
4. Release the bubble, and see it soar higher and higher into the heavens, until it is absorbed into glowing light.
5. You are reinstated again in the wonderful security and peace you enjoy when you surrender to your Higher Self. Bask in the confidence of knowing your problems are in the capable care of a power higher than yourself.
6. Visualize yourself skipping happily along a broad, straight highway, moving freely and directly to your goals. See yourself protected and guided, surrounded by brilliant light.

* * * * * * * * * * * * * * * * * *

You may surrender control of yourself to Higher Intelligence at any time. If you forget to do so upon awakening, just stop for a moment during the day and make that commitment. Should you slip back temporarily into the stressful realm of your Lower Self, again just take a few quiet moments to re-establish harmony with your Higher Self. With experience it will become simple and easy, a brief pause while you attune yourself and experience the buoyant shift into blitheness and ease which signals the change.

Over and over again, the magnanimous guidance of your divine Higher Self will gently manifest itself in ways wondrous beyond imagination. Your dips into lesser awareness will become infrequent and inconsequential, quickly recognized and easily remedied. Soon this state of joyous communication and lightness will be your normal condition.

SECTION III

SPREADING THE LIGHT

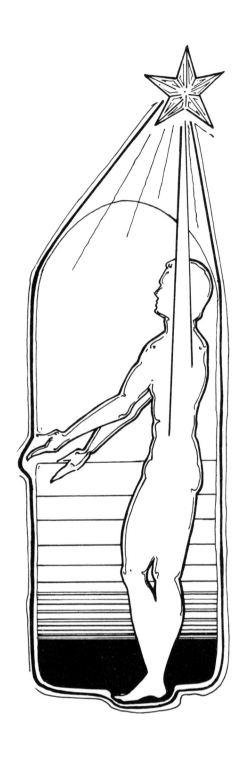

CHAPTER 14
WHITE LIGHT

In this chapter you will be shown some of the most
important techniques in the realm of metaphysical
studies, skills which were protected and guarded in the
past.

In preceding chapters you learned that thoughts are real,
potent with possibilities for good or ill. With the following
processes you will use thoughts to elevate the atmosphere of
your environment, to bring healing and energy to yourself
and others, and to surround yourself with total protection so
that nothing can harm you. You will be working with the
central, most significant principle of transformation, the
ineffable power and magic of light.

Light is an integral part of every esoteric study, mentioned
in the basic scriptures of all religions. Many of us are familiar
with descriptions of light recorded in the Bible. For example:
"Ye are the children of light." (Thessalonians V, 5)
"There shone from heaven a great light around me."
(Acts XXVI, 13)
"Let us put on the armour of light." (Romans XIII, 12)
"Your whole body is full of light." (Luke II, 34)
"Walk in light as He is in the light." (John I, 07)
"Let your light so shine before men that they may see
your good works." (Matthew V, 16)
"While ye have light, believe in the light, that ye may be
the children of light." (John XII, 36)
Often we express these references symbolically in our
everyday speech, such as:
"The light dawned on him."

"Suddenly I saw the light."
"The light of understanding."
However, these scriptural references are meant to be taken literally. They are describing light itself: brilliant, blazing, luminous light.

If you are learning to meditate, you may pass through a period when you sense beautiful colors with your inner vision, hues which shimmer and glow. Later you may begin to perceive bright white light, sometimes as flashes from your peripheral vision, sometimes as a glow over your head. You are attuning to higher rates of vibration, to energy just beyond your present range of perception.

As you study and practice the esoteric disciplines, you expand the range of your inner senses. Soon you will be able to distinguish form where you previously saw only light. At the outer limits of your perception you will experience as light still higher rates of vibration. For you are beginning to contact the realms of light, the spiritual dimensions.

Since with our thoughts we create, we can immerse ourselves in white light just by visualizing. We do not have to wait until we have attained the inner growth such spontaneous flashes of light represent; we can draw to ourselves the benefits of light by imagining it.

When we visualize ourselves surrounded by white light, this high vibratory rate will of itself act as a passageway to higher realms of consciousness. We can attune to our superconscious selves by imagining white light and surrounding ourselves with its radiance.

Consider for a moment the magnitude of this statement. By the mere act of visualizing, you can raise your consciousness from the mundane world and instantaneously lift into higher realms of being.

You have no need for rigid discipline nor arduous preparation, only the ability to quiet your thought processes enough to permit clear and unobstructed imaging of light. Merely by thinking, you open the doors to the spiritual dimension and project yourself there.

As you become increasingly competent at relaxing and working with light, you will eliminate the need for additional techniques and disciplines. The Light itself will be the means of your further evolvement into higher consciousness.

Within the white light you are visualizing is contained enormous power. This is the light of protection, the light of healing, the light of love, the Christ Light. You will learn to attune to this white light and to apply its potency through exercises which may seem deceptively simple. Yet this technique is one of the most cherished secrets of all the ages.

As part of the exercises, you will picture yourself surrounded with a bubble of light, encircling yourself with an energy field of very high vibratory rate. Higher rates of vibration negate and overpower lower rates of vibration, just as high voltage in an electrical transmission line will overpower one of lesser voltage.

Whenever you feel yourself in need of protection of any nature, whether physical, emotional, mental or psychic, close your eyes and imagine yourself totally enveloped in a great bubble of brilliant white light. Nothing of a lower nature can penetrate this shield of light, whatever its source or form.

The use of white light for protection is possibly the most widely used of all the metaphysical arts. It is easy to do and dramatically effective. We may even underestimate its potency because of its very simplicity, yet a few personal experiences will usually evoke a deep respect for its power.

Many people place their vehicles inside a field of white light whenever they are driving. It is not unusual for such protected drivers to escape collision, for anything which threatens to strike them seems to bounce off the surrounding energy field as surely as if it had hit a physical barrier. Those who experience such first-hand evidence of the protective power of light are quickly convinced that they drive in an island of total safety.

You may also use white light to neutralize any negative forces you may encounter. These forces are very real and can embody great power. Through the centuries, many of those who have understood the laws of energy have misused their knowledge unlawfully to manipulate and control other people. One simple method for neutralizing discordant energy, one used frequently by healers and body therapists, is to discharge it into the ground. You will be learning another method which will not only cleanse and negate energy, but can actually transform it into positive, beneficial power.

Part of this technique will involve the mental creation of a five-pointed star within your aura. Its continuing presence there will facilitate attunement to your higher guidance, for it is a symbol of what is sometimes called the "Christ Light."

By visualizing a star over your head, you actually magnetize higher energy and consciousness to yourself. You can then project this loving power to all in need, serving humanity proficiently yet unobtrusively as you go about your daily affairs.

The next exercise has several goals: protection, cleansing, healing, and projecting light. It is a basic, powerful technique, one which you will find applicable to many areas of your life.

Exercise 1 — The Star and Bubble of Light

1. Enter your meditative level by your deep relaxation technique.
2. Create in your imagination a brilliant white star, a five-pointed star with one point directed straight upward. Imagine this star suspended from 30 to 60 inches above your head, radiating and pulsing light.
3. Next imagine a great bubble around your body.
4. Project a beam of light from the star through the top of your head, letting it move slowly and evenly downward, gradually filling your entire body.
5. See the light pushing all darkness and negativity out of your body, emptying through the soles of your feet, into a container beneath you.

6. When all of the darkness is removed, and your body is filled with light, seal the container and project it far out into space.
7. See the container of negativity struck by lightning, and in a great shower of brilliance, reduced to its shimmering elements.
8. Now visualize the light flowing out from your feet, circulating within the bubble, and again entering your body through your head. Let the beams from the star maintain a constant inpouring of white light, filling and surrounding you with luminosity.
9. Imagine a great beacon of light projecting from the center of your forehead, another beam from the base of your throat, a third beam from your heart, and two additional light beams from the centers of your palms.
10. You are filled and surrounded with light; radiating, channeling, projecting light; the light of healing, the light of protection, the light of love, the Christ Light.

* * * * * * * * * * * * * * * * * * * *

This is a valuable exercise to do each morning soon after awakening. Take a few minutes to relax, enter your meditative state, visualize the star and bubble, the beams of light filling the bubble and your body, the great beacons radiating out. You will be filled with energy and vitality and a wonderful sense of well-being.

Wherever you go during the day, you will radiate light, affecting all whom you encounter. When you sit or stand beside another person, or pass him on the street, he will receive light from you. You may change a person's life without saying a word.

In Biblical lore, a woman was instantly healed when she merely touched the hem of Jesus's garment and encountered the intense healing power of His energy field (Matthew 9, 20-22). You are working with the same power. You are "letting your light shine forth into the world."

White Light and Energy Interchange

We can observe this exchange when we study auras. If we examine the auras of two people sitting apart, then ask them to sit together, we will see the auric colors blend and merge. We are all part of each other, influencing and being influenced by everyone we meet.

This exchange can create a problem for those with normal or high energy who are in touch with those of low energy. Whenever you spend time in a room with other people, the energy level in the room will balance within twenty minutes. If you are filled with abundant vitality when you enter a roomful of people who are depressed, angry, or ill, they will soon be more cheerful and energetic, while you are wondering what has happened to you; why you are suddenly weary and fatigued, the joy drained from your day.

When you fill yourself with light before entering the room, however, the results are entirely different. Your impact will be felt as soon as you enter, and within twenty minutes all of those in the room will be in your same high level of energy.

Because you are channeling light, drawing upon reserves of energy outside yourself, you will keep your own energy field intact, with no danger of depletion or drain. You will also be protected from absorbing lower emotions from others, since higher rates of vibration, or higher emotions, repel lower rates of vibrations or emotions. You will be unaffected by the anger or depression of other people.

White Light and Healing

You may consciously project this powerful light to anyone whom you judge to be in need of healing or encouragement, whether you know him or not. Just imagine the beams of light radiating from your head, throat, or heart, projecting to this person and surrounding him with light.

His own Higher Self will modulate and absorb all of the

light he can assimilate and use at the time, and will store the rest of his further enrichment. You may observe sudden changes in this person's demeanor and bearing — he will act as if he had just awakened from a dream. It is part of his karma, or life path, that the two of you have met, and part of yours to have this opportunity to serve. You might feel somewhat conspicuous if you raise your hands to project light, so reserve this additional source of power for those occasions when you are comfortable using it.

Energy Drainers

A special problem, of serious concern to students of parapsychology, are those individuals who cannot retain their own psychic energy, and consequently drain too much from other people. Perhaps some of your friends or family members have this condition, as it is widespread.

You can recognize such energy drainers by your own subjective reactions; you will feel weary and depleted whenever you are with them. You may even become exhausted just by talking to them on the telephone. Some patients in mental hospitals are especially prone to this disorder. It may also temporarily affect normally healthy people in certain circumstances.

The following analogy may be useful for understanding the cause of this problem. Each of us is like a small ship bobbing about in a great sea, secured from the elements by strong protective walls of steel. Our walls, however, are composed of the energy of light, which differentiates us in the sea of consciousness. One of our most precious resources is this shield of light which enables us to remain separate entities, sealing us away from the surrounding waters of extraneous energy, discordant forces and thought forms.

People who drain energy from others have breached their own natural protective shields; somehow they have blown holes in their auras. Whenever we surrender control of

ourselves, or relinquish dominion of our own being to a
lesser power, we court the danger of rupturing the shield.
This surrender may be accidental or deliberate.
Periods of unconsciousness from injury, a blow on the
head, or general anaesthesia, may open the aura. Any
intense negative emotion, such as fear or rage, can also rip
open this protective energy field; anger is particularly
destructive to the inner planes. Extremely loud and jarring
noises may disrupt the aura as well.

Perhaps the most common causes of damage to the
protective shield are alcohol and drugs, prescription drugs as
well as street narcotics.

Be wary of any substances or circumstances which result
in abnormal loss of self-control, which expose you to lower
energies or forces. Normal sleep and meditation, of course,
are safe and beneficial ways of relinquishing control to the
only control allowable, the Higher Self.

Students of parapsychology and metaphysics learn many
ways of protecting themselves from psychic energy drainers,
but few are taught means of helping or curing those who
drain this energy from others. You may correct this
condition for another by applying the same technique you
have used for yourself, as follows:

Exercise 2 — Assisting Psychic Drainers

1. Imagine a five-pointed star with one point directed
   upward, thirty inches above the subject's head.
2. Surround him with a great bubble of light.
3. Imagine beams of light filling both the bubble and the
   subject's body with brilliant light.
4. See light pouring out the person's feet and circulating
   within the bubble.
5. As light builds up in intensity, imagine great searchlights
   projecting from the center of the subject's forehead, the
   base of his throat, his heart and the center of each of his
   palms.

6. You may add an extra layer of protection to his aura by covering the recipient's bubble with an outer coating of indigo blue (a deep purplish blue). Indigo is the color of protection, an additional armour which will exclude anything of a lower vibration and admit only higher frequencies.
7. Establish the star and bubble as permanent and indestructable.

* * * * * * * * * * * * * * * * * * *

Use this technique to channel extra energy to other people during crises or times of specific need. Nearly everyone benefits from an influx of light, so you may wish to send light occasionally in this manner, as a special gift to those most dear to you.

On a daily basis, fill your home with light, as well as other rooms and places you enter. You will change the whole atmosphere of your surroundings.

Exercise 3 — Filling your Home and Workplace with Light

1. Stand in the doorway and imagine light flooding a room, dissolving all darkness and discord.
2. Feel it pouring through you, projecting from your hands, your heart, your throat and your forehead.
3. Concentrate light in your office or workshop, and around your desk.
4. If you work in an area which is part of a larger room, fill the entire room with light, then focus an extra amount of light in your own private section.

* * * * * * * * * * * * * * * * * * *

Observe the changes which usually begin to occur immediately. People will react to the brightness, the joyousness and peace which accompany the light. They will feel as if they had discovered an oasis in an otherwise arid world. Your own work and relationships will have a new harmony and zest. You may have difficulty persuading people to leave; they will want to bask in the energy around you.

Some occupations have a greater need for light than do others. Those who work in the healing arts, in counseling and social services, and those who work with controversy or discord may find this technique especially beneficial. They need it first for their own protection, to be able to give of themselves without depletion, and secondly for the power and aid they can channel to others.

People who work with illness can transform a hospital or treatment center. Nurses have experimented with standing quietly in the doorway of each patient's room for a few minutes, filling the room with light, then moving to the next room. They are rewarded with an amazing emotional uplift, accelerated healing, a mellowness and general air of happiness which pervade the entire center.

Attorneys and arbitrators describe harmony, smoother reconciliation of differences, and lessening of hostilities in rooms which have been treated with light. Some quietly fill a courtroom with light before a trial.

Performing the light exercise as a routine habit each morning upon awakening will fortify you in all your activities during the day. However, you may bring in light at any time, whenever you have need for additional protection or power. You may wish to do an abbreviated version during the day:

Exercise 4 — Abbreviated White Light Protection

1. Imagine the star over your head.
2. Imagine the bubble surrounding you, the beams from the star filling the bubble with light, but let your body fill with light rapidly, without the special clearing action.
3. Increase the intensity quickly, and create the outpouring beams almost immediately.

4. This exercise is a valuable source of instant energy and protection. With practice, you will be able to leave your eyes open and instantly visualize yourself completely filled with light, projecting goodwill to all you meet, at any time or place, in any circumstances.

* * * * * * * * * * * * * * * * * * * *

We have been considering ways in which white light may be used in daily life. There are other uses for light applications, which involve greater power and impact.

Following a cosmic design, we first put our individual houses in order, by learning to master and govern our own lives. We are then able to direct our energies and efforts with clarity and power to the betterment of mankind.

Whenever you meditate, spend a few moments sending love and energy to the earth and to humanity. This is a beautiful way to conclude the white light exercise.

Exercise 5 — Healing the World with Light

1. In your meditative level, imagine the five-pointed star over your head; see it increasing in brilliance and magnitude.
2. If you are meditating with a group, be aware of the stars over their heads. As your stars expand, feel them blend and merge into one single immense, magnificent star, and feel yourself united and one with them.
3. Then imagine yourselves with your star out in space, thousands of miles away from our planet, and look back at the earth, our glowing, beautiful Mother Earth.
4. From your star, project a powerful beam of intense white light, filling and surrounding the earth and all those upon the earth with luminosity. See every particle of the earth and those upon the earth irradiated, aligned, attuned, vibrant with light.
5. Then looking down, notice any special areas of darkness

upon the earth, any clouds of negativity. Send powerful
beams of light to dissolve each scar of darkness; see them
dissipate and melt away.
6. With the earth cleansed and clear, project a great beam
   of golden light, flooding the earth and those upon the
   earth with gold. . . . gold the color of blessing, the color
   of the new age. Be aware of the great star above you, and
   the canopy of golden light enfolding you, immersing you
   in blessing.
7. Conclude your meditation and bring yourself out in your
   usual manner.

* *

The regular use of this exercise will have a more profound
and far-reaching effect than you can realize. All over the
world, dedicated individuals and groups are pouring light
and love into the earth in one way or another. They are
helping to raise the vibratory level of the earth, cancelling
the enormous burden of negativity and misused energy
which has afflicted the human race because of its actions of
the past.

All of us who join this endeavor are assisting the earth and
humanity through the process of transition to higher
consciousness, making it possible to enter the new age
gently, smoothly, without turbulence or destruction. As you
work with the light, you become part of this critical venture,
helping more than you can possibly imagine, to hasten that
transition into a glorious new state of being.

CHAPTER 15
MEETING YOUR
SPIRITUAL GUIDES

Now you are ready for the beautiful ceremony in which you will meet your spiritual guides! You have probably wondered and speculated about these mysterious beings; are they fact or fancy, myth or legend? For even though other people may see and describe their guides, yours will have no true reality for you until you have personally felt their presence and established direct communication with them.

When you have completed the ceremony of introduction in this chapter, you will not only have established contact with your guides, but henceforth you will be able to reach them consciously at any time you desire. Through this new avenue of communication, they will counsel and protect you, instruct and inspire you, will open new doorways to knowledge and wisdom. They are very real beings, whose presence will delight you and enhance the quality of your life.

Since you are always accompanied by one or more invisible guardians, you are never really alone. They manifest on many different levels, overseeing your every possible need or interest.

You have guides who are protectors, those who are concerned with your health, others who help with your career, your relationships, your plans and your dreams. You have special counselors who are guardian angels and high spiritual masters.

Perhaps you are totally oblivious of their existence, or again you may occasionally sense their presence. You may already share a close personal communion. Whether or not you perceive their presence, they are always near.

Who are these guides? Why are they with us? So many sources have confirmed their existence that we no longer question their actuality. . . . instead we ponder their purpose and origin.

Are they, perhaps, as some psychologists suggest, aspects of our own Higher Selves, personified? Or is there possibly another interpretation which might better explain the prevailing feeling of exile from a bright homeland which is felt by so many seekers, a compelling sense of commitment to a vital personal mission?

Many of these seekers have suggested the following explanation, which for them is deeply reassuring, with the comfortable ring of truth:

We are emissaries for the manifestation of Higher Consciousness upon the earth, blessed with physical bodies which enable us to function upon this plane. When we are born into the world, we voluntarily leave behind the realms of light, and submerge ourselves in the slow, heavy vibrations of the earthly plane. As we descend, a veil is drawn, shielding us from memories of our former existence. This shielding is essential, for even though we volunteered to come, few of us would elect to remain in such discord if we retained clear recollection of the radiance we left behind.

However, we have not been abandoned to solitary quests, for a large assemblage of beings accompanies each of us. These are guardians and guides, working with us and through us, but remaining at finer vibratory levels, in touch with both realms of existence. Each assemblage is entrusted with a specific assignment, and we in our human bodies are the captains who determine, through our free will, the success or failure of each mission.

Our guardians nurture us through myriad stages of growth, as we learn to master our lower natures, and to gradually perfect the attunement linking our Lesser Selves with our Higher Selves.

Once we have established direct contact with our Higher Selves and with Universal Consciousness, a major aspect of their task is completed. Henceforth our guidance comes directly from Higher Consciousness. Our guides will step into the background, still inspiring and protecting us, but indirectly rather than overtly.

In the ceremony, your guides may appear to you in almost any guise. You may see them as radiant, mystical beings, or they may assume more familiar, less exotic appearances. They will present themselves to you in forms which are meaningful and acceptable to you at this time.

They may manifest as adults, children, as beings from other planets or dimensions. They may be people you know, casual acquaintances or intimate members of your family. They may appear as persons who are no longer on the earth plane, frequently as parents or grandparents.

They can be celebrities, famous individuals from the past or present. They may be high spiritual beings, such as Moses, John the Baptist, Krishna or Confucious. Each guide has his own distinct personality, and is a definite individual in his own right.

Sometimes a person meeting his guides for the first time will sense a presence but will not see a definite form. He may see colors or lights, or will just have an impression that someone is there. This is an indication that he is tuning into one of his higher teachers. He is unable to distinguish form because he has not yet perfected his ability to perceive such high vibrations. If his inner sense of hearing is beginning to develop, he may hear the voices of his guides instead of seeing their faces.

Those who are unable either to see or to hear their guides will usually sense their presence through a highly sensitive instinct of "knowing". They do not hear answers to questions, but will just "know" the answers. This is actually a much higher method of communication. Most people who communicate regularly with their guides go through stages of visualizing and hearing them, then graduate to the stage of knowing without perceiving form or voice.

If this is your experience, you may rejoice in the knowledge that you have reached a high level of communication with your master teachers. Their counseling will thrill you with its beauty and accuracy.

However, perhaps you would feel more confidence with a guide whom you could visualize or hear, one with a more tangible form. If this is the case, then simply create a form. Imagine any personality you wish, such as a flamenco dancer, a Viking or a Roman senator.

When you have developed a satisfactory image, pause for a moment to consider your selection. Out of all possibilities, why did you decide to create those specific characteristics? Where do creativity and imagination originate. . . . from what source does inspiration flow? Higher Intelligence will communicate with you through any vehicle which is provided, whether it appears spontaneously or whether you "make it up".

Guides Can Appear in Many Forms

Frequently the features of a guide's face seem to change, sometimes assuming many forms. This apparently indicates that several guides are eager to meet you and are attempting to come through. If this should happen, select the one with the clearest features, and the others will disappear. Later you may bring in other guides, but it is best to begin by establishing rapport with a single male and female before contacting others.

Guides sometimes identify themselves with a sound, a touch or an odor. Often a guide announces his presence by a distinctive perfume which may be sensed by others in the room. For example, the exquisite scent of roses usually accompanies St. Theresa, the Little Flower, who frequently appears as counselor for those who are spiritual healers.

The finer vibrations of higher beings usually stimulate a resonance which meditators perceive in various ways. Sometimes they feel a gentle touch on their shoulders or the tops of their heads; often they feel flooded with intense heat, or they may see brilliant white or violet light. Sometimes a reader is reluctant to accept a guide who is legendary or renown. He may ask himself humbly, "Who am I that Leonardo da Vinci should come to me as a guide?" Such well-known individuals do appear as guides, and are not just responses to our own yearnings.

On the other hand, a reader may anticipate that his guide will be someone for whom he feels a special rapport. His expectation may be realized, or someone totally different may appear.

Many people in our culture meet Jesus as a spiritual guide. Those who are clairsentient frequently experience a very special feeling in their hearts whenever they communicate with Him, a joyous effervescence which announces His presence. Those who are less sensitive to feelings may experience Him in other ways, perhaps as light or voice or form, but a deep outpouring of love is reported by most of those who meet Him.

The introduction of inner teachers is usually a beautiful, exalted experience. Occasionally, however, someone may feel uncomfortable with a guide, usually for one of the following reasons:

1. The student has permitted worldly concerns or negative emotions to intrude upon the sanctity of the ceremony.
2. His teacher has appeared in a form exemplifying necessary but unwelcome lessons which the recipient would rather avoid.

Preparation For the Ceremony of Meeting Your Guides

The ceremony of meeting your guides will be quite different from anything else we have been doing. We will approach the ceremony with respect and solemnity. Proper preparation is essential, so select a time when you are free from other distractions, when your mood is tranquil and harmonious.

In the exercise you will again attune yourself to your radiant star and surround yourself with white light. This will protect the reverence of your meditation, for it will create a force-field of such high frequency that lower vibrations cannot intrude.

However, you yourself can breach that shield if you permit your thoughts to stray to worldly concerns or to distracting emotional issues of your outer life. If you focus your attention upon mundane affairs during the exercise, you may carry these lower feelings with you into the purity of your sanctuary.

You may then have the surprising experience of seeing those feelings and thoughts personified, graphically revealing their true nature. They may appear as funny, scurrying little creatures, as gargoyles or strange beings with homely visages. They are your own creations, your own darker thoughts and emotions pictorially exposed.

Simply command them to leave, and they will obediently disappear. Then take a few minutes to acknowledge the lesson they were demonstrating, and compose yourself, lifting your thoughts to more ethereal realms.

The guides who appear to you are here to help you with the specific issues and lessons important in your life at this time. We do not always welcome those lessons which are essential, so may wish to reject them when we encounter them so vividly portrayed.

You are in complete charge of yourself and your workshop on these dimensions; you have the power and privilege of refusing entry to any beings who may appear. However, unless you are unusually uncomfortable with a guide, accept his presence and assistance while you learn the lessons he is to teach.

Your guides are often visible to people who are clairvoyant and have the ability to see auras. Perhaps these clairvoyants discern light or a luminous glow above you, or may actually distinguish your counselor's features and forms. Another clairvoyant may later describe the same guide, or he may attune to a totally different being. Usually a prominent guide will be with you for a considerable period of time, until you have learned the lessons he is presenting. He may then depart, to be replaced by another. Many guides may come and go throughout your lifetime, but all are ultimately the servants of your own Higher Self, the spark of divinity indwelling your consciousness.

Exercise: Creating your Sanctuary

You will meet your guides in a very beautiful, special ceremony. This is one exercise which is best done with a group of friends who meditate or study with you, since the energy of a group will enhance your own experience. You may do it privately, of course, if a group is unavailable. With a group or by yourself, choose a time when you can be assured of privacy, quiet yourself and begin:

1. Descend to your meditative level, and enter your workshop.
2. Spend a few moments in meditation and reflection, so you feel peaceful and attuned.
3. Be aware of the five-pointed star over your head, the radiant star with one point pointing upward. Feel the great bubble of light around you, the beams of light projecting from you.
4. Now in your imagination create an elevator, placing it on your south wall.
5. When it is completed, enter the elevator. The door closes behind you and the elevator begins to ascend.
6. You feel yourself rising higher and higher, far above the workshop level. The elevator stops, the door opens, and you move outside into a large corridor.

7. Before you is a tall, handsome door. Approach the door, open it and step inside.
8. You are in a room filled with vibrancy and lightness, a beautiful area conducive to communication with Higher Consciousness, your sanctuary.
9. Design and decorate your sanctuary, using fabrics and furnishings which surround you with beauty. Consider music, lighting, and colors which inspire feelings of upliftment and harmony. In the center, create an altar.
10. When your sanctuary is complete, pause for a few moments of meditation to absorb its peaceful atmosphere.

* * * * * * * * * * * * * * * * * * * *

With a feeling of reverence, prepare yourself for the beautiful ceremony in which you will meet your spiritual guides. As the ceremony begins to unfold, progress at your own rate, pausing to experience fully.

Exercise: Meeting your Guides

1. Imagine now a great golden stairway rising from your sanctuary and lifting to infinity. See yourself standing, facing the stairway.
2. In the mists at the top of the stairs a light begins to shimmer and glow, then starts to move slowly downward. It becomes larger and more brilliant as it descends, gradually revealing itself as a tall column of shining light.
3. As it draws closer, you begin to distinguish first a male outline and then his attire.
4. The figure pauses, enabling you to observe his raiment, his historical period and nationality.
5. He approaches to stand directly before you, a short distance away.

6. The glow around his head gradually begins to form into features, becoming more and more distinct, until you see his face clearly.
7. Study his face closely, noticing the color of his hair, the shape of his nose, his mouth, his ears.
8. When you have a clear impression or image of your male guide, invite him to come closer, and move forward to meet him.
9. Greet him, ask him his name, his special purpose in being with you at this time. What are the lessons he is to teach you? Welcome him. Spend some time becoming acquainted with him.
10. He may be warm and welcoming, or reserved and aloof. Each guide has his own distinct personality, his own individuality. Your relationship will become more intimate as you work together, as you perfect your ability to attune to these higher levels.

    He is in touch with Higher Consciousness, here to help and guide you, to assist you in all the affairs of your life. Through his attunement to Infinite Intelligence he will be able to answer any questions you may ask, a dependable source of knowledge and wisdom.
11. Visit with him as long as you like. When you feel that you are ready to continue the ceremony, he will join you in meeting your female counselor.

Meeting Your Female Counselor

1. Stand with your male counselor beside you, facing the long golden stairway.
2. At the top of the stairs, a light begins to glow, dimly at first, then brighter and brighter as it descends. It shimmers into a column of brilliant light, then glowingly reveals a feminine form.
3. The being pauses, giving you an opportunity to observe her clothing, her historical period, her nationality.
4. Then as the figure moves closer, you are able to

distinguish the features, the hair, the nose, the mouth, and then the eyes of your feminine counselor.

5. When you feel that you have a clear image or impression, invite her to come forward, and advance to meet her.

6. Welcome her, ask her her name, her special purpose in being with you at this time. What is she to teach you? How is she to help you? Spend some time becoming acquainted with her.

7. She is a wonderful advisor and teacher, here to assist you and your male counselor in all of your interests and activities. Often your guides will inform you that each is to help you in specific aspects of your life.

8. When you are ready to conclude the meeting, your guides will accompany you down the elevator into your workshop.

9. Conduct a brief farewell ceremony or prayer, one you will use each time you part in the future. Later you will create a welcoming prayer or ceremony, to be used each time you enter your workshop or meet your guides.

10. From now on, your guides will be there to greet you whenever you enter your workshop. You may communicate with them at any time just by desiring to do so.

11. When you have said your farewells, bring yourself out in your usual manner, feeling joyous and happy, grounded and in harmony with all of life.

* * * * * * * * * * * * * * * * * * *

When you have worked with your guides for several weeks, you will probably be ready to meet other guides. You may repeat the ceremony, by yourself or even better with a group.

Often your present guides will leave when the new ones appear, indicating that you have learned the lessons they were to teach. Or they may remain as you welcome the new guides, and you will have the pleasure of working with all of them.

When your guides eventually leave you, this too is part of the pattern, part of the goal: to study, learn and grow with your nurturing inner teachers, then to step beyond this stage, leaving them behind as you communicate directly with your own High Self.

This is the constant focus of their guidance and direction, as it is with every true teacher. A teacher succeeds when the student outgrows his need for the teacher, when the student leaves to journey alone, mature and self-confident, secure in the knowledge which he has attained.

But now your guides are with you as loving companions, an unceasing source of inspiration, stimulation and delight.

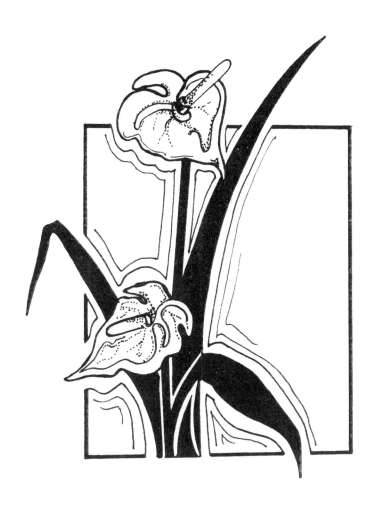

CHAPTER 16
THE INNER WORLD
OF GEMS AND FLOWERS,
MINERALS AND PLANTS

L
ike most of us, you are probably but dimly aware of the innate intelligence inherent in the three major kingdoms of nature, which coexist with humanity upon the earth: the mineral, the plant life and the animal kingdoms. Even though we are all interconnected and interdependent through the grand scheme of life itself, the majority of us know the intricacies of these other kingdoms only through objective observation.

Now, however, you will begin to examine these realms of nature from a new perspective, as you learn to share their energies intimately and to resonate with the very essence of their beings. You will be delving into areas inaccessible to the outer senses, using techniques which will develop your imagination and inner senses.

You will be projecting your awareness into atomic, molecular and organic levels as you explore the structures and functioning of these intriguing worlds which complement our own. Your methods of perception will be uniquely individual and consistent, differing from the responses of others, as your imagination carries you safely through dimensions of indescribable color, beauty and design.

You will discover the fascination of exploring gemstones, rocks, woods, metals, and various species of plant life from the cellular and molecular levels as well as from the vibrational, energy levels.

Later you will study the skeletal structure and internal organs of your own pets, pinpointing areas which have been causing health problems, and sending energy to correct those problems. You can direct your consciousness to any level of being and experience that level both as a participant and as an observer.

Your trips of exploration will begin with journeys into the mineral kingdom, into rocks, metals, crystals, minerals and gemstones.

Exercise: Exploring the Mineral Kingdom

1. Select an object such as a crystal, and using all of your normal outer senses, make a close study of that object. Examine it closely with your hands, noticing the texture and feeling. Be aware of any odor or fragrance, as you hold it close to your face to study details. Then set it aside.
2. Now close your eyes, relax, and enter your deep meditative level.
3. Mentally examine the crystal with your inner senses just as you did with the outer. However, in addition to mentally picturing your hands holding the crystal, actually use your hands physically to feel and sense its form. You will re-experience the same sensations and feelings that you felt previously when you were physically holding the object.
4. Again use your physical hand to bring the imagined object close to your face, visualizing its details mentally just as you observed them when you studied it with your outer vision.
5. When you feel that you have created a clear and vivid impression, touch your forehead with your hand. Then mentally project your consciousness and your senses inside the object.
6. You may picture yourself as barely fitting within the crystal, or you may imagine that you are inside a huge

room, or you may find that you are a tiny being inhabiting an enormous structure. Let your imagination flow, enjoying the impressions you receive.

7. When you are ready to return, touch your forehead again and tell yourself that you are now coming out of the crystal.

8. You are suddenly aware of yourself back in your chair, once more your normal size, mentally holding the crystal in your hand.

9. Physically and mentally extend your arm, release the crystal to float in space, command it to disappear, and see it vanish.

10. Bring yourself back in your usual manner, feeling happy, refreshed, in tune with life.

* * * * * * * * * * * * * * * * * * * *

Later you may repeat the exercise, exploring a variety of minerals, and noticing the completely different impressions you will perceive with each. Your impressions, however, will be consistent whenever you repeat projections into the same types of minerals.

When you have examined several varieties of stones and minerals, you are ready to venture into the inner world of the plant life kingdom.

Exercise: Inner Exploration of the Plant Life Kingdom

1. Select a leaf for a first subject, one still attached to its plant. Examine it carefully, using all your outer senses, sensing its texture, its fragrance, its color and design. Study it from a distance and close to your face. Then set it aside.

2. Close your eyes, relax, and enter your meditative level. Now examine the leaf with your inner senses just as you did with your outer. Use your physical hands to develop the added dimensions of extended touch, repeating the

physical gestures you used in your initial exploration. Mentally observe it close to your face and from afar.

3. Now touch your forehead with your physical and mental hand, and project yourself into the leaf. Again, you may find yourself snugly filling the whole leaf, or you may be a miniscule being in a vast new world.

4. Be aware of the energy field around you. Do you sense movement? Notice the special feeling of the life force.

5. How is the humidity? The light. . . . the colors? Do you smell a fragrance? Do you hear a sound? Listen!

6. When you feel that you are ready to return, touch your forehead with your physical hand and tell yourself that you are now coming out of the leaf. You feel yourself back in your chair, your normal size, mentally holding the leaf in your hand.

7. Physically and mentally extend your arm, release the leaf to float in space, then command it to disappear, and watch it vanish. Bring yourself back in your usual manner.

* * * * * * * * * * * * * * * * * * * *

When you repeat the exercise, broaden your repertoire by including many kinds of leaves, flowers, plants and trees. Study them in different stages of growth: budding, in full bloom, bearing fruit, forming seeds. Experience springtime shoots, plants which are sere and withered; be one with the soaring redwoods, the desert cacti, the arctic tundra.

In this inner world of the plant life kingdom, you might find yourself carried along in a tumultuous stream, struggling through a forest of stamens, dazzled by a spinning world of atoms, or rocked gently in velvety petals. Your experience can be infinitely varied as a whole new microcosm awaits your exploration.

When you feel the life force coursing through the capillaries of leaves and flowers, you will be touching an exultant power far different from the stolid energy in stones.

Yet the mineral kingdom reveals limitless variations within its span of vibratory manifestations.

Sense the intense, coarser energy of quartz crystals as contrasted with the ordered, concentrated energy in diamonds and other fine gemstones. You may attune yourself to the special pulsing energy in gold, a distinction which has made gold univerally treasured by those intuitive races who could sense the subtle vibrations.

As you experiment, you will develop deep respect for the intelligence and consciousness inherent in other kingdoms and levels of being.

Imagine the wonderful new frontiers which are yours to explore, the limitless applications of your newly discovered insight. Miners, prospectors, geologists find such abilities of inestimable value in their search to discover and evaluate mineral and oil deposits within the earth.

When you have established reference points for different metals and gemstones, you will find it easy to identify unfamiliar metals and gemstones, simple to check them for composition and authenticity.

Once you have tuned in to metals and minerals, you may explore the inner dimensions of anything made of metal. You will no doubt find many opportunities to apply your skills in everyday life, as your encounters with typewriters, sewing machines, refrigerators and mixers become smooth and well-lubricated. Use your new sensitivities for analysis, but acknowledge also the consciousness within each unit.

Exercise: Attuning to your Car

One rewarding project you will probably undertake quickly is learning to attune to your car.

1. Enter your workshop level with your usual method.
2. Place your car upon your mental screen. Ask to be shown any areas of potential difficulties.

3. Program that some special signal, such as an imaginary flashing red light, will indicate areas needing attention.
4. You will become expert in locating the source of unusual noises, in discovering the causes of mechanical problems.
5. Establish a pattern of scanning your car periodically, of singing in harmony and rhythm with the motor as you travel.

* * * * * * * * * * * * * * * * * * * *

You will probably never again run out of fuel, have an unexpected flat tire, nor have a major breakdown. Your car will seem to respond and cooperate with the harmonious rapport you have established.

You have learned through these exercises that you may project your awareness into objects and plants, concentrating your focus at the microscopic level as you analyze and scrutinize their inner design. You may also expand your awareness in other directions, projecting your consciousness to exotic and unusual realms which you may now comfortably share.

For example, view the world from the top of a swaying tree, plumb the green and luminous life in the depths of the sea, experience the lushness of a tropical jungle, explore crystalline caves far below the surface of the earth.

Through projection and imagination, the entire cosmos is your home, yours to claim in total safety and security.

Simply enter your intuitive level, surround and fill yourself with light, then use your inner screen as your magic carpet, put on your seven-league boots and explore.

CHAPTER 17
THE INNER WORLD
OF ANIMALS

You can communicate with animals! Just as you have explored the inner worlds of the mineral and plant life kingdoms, you can in the same manner explore the inner world of the animal kingdom.

Many of us have studied our pets, the birds and the wild creatures of the field and pondered with regret the inviolate barrier which seems to separate us from them. Most of these creatures seem to have a mutual bond, an intimacy and flow of communication which links them together in an understanding which excludes only Man.

Now, however, your new level of awareness will enable you to dissolve those barriers. You are ready to open the doors to this hidden kingdom, ready to establish your own ties and channels of communication with other species. You will be fulfilling an ages-old dream of mankind when you do.

You have earned this precious privilege because you have learned to attune consciously to your intuitive level of awareness, the same frequency which animals use to communicate with one another. You are "tuning in to their wave-lengths".

Our North American Indians have long understood the secret of non-verbal communication; they once taught every child the art of communing with nature. Animals were treated with loving respect. When Indians wished to communicate with animals, they projected beams of light from their hearts to the animals' hearts. They were working with white light just as you are now working with light.

In the following exercises, you will learn first to view the anatomy of an animal as if you had X-Ray vision. You will be able to determine if there are any imperfections, imbalances or injuries, able to observe the energy patterns, the harmonies of this beautiful manifestation of life. Equally as exciting, you will be able to converse mentally with your pets, bridging the gap of understanding between the human and animal worlds.

When you practiced the exercises of projecting your awareness into various types of minerals and plants, you were laying a foundation which will enable you to explore higher forms of life, and to move from the simple to the more complex.

In the following exercises, imagine that your hands are made of light, able to touch lightly and to bless whatever they touch.

Exercise: Attuning to an Animal

1. Enter your intuitive level in your usual manner. Imagine your inner visual screen.
2. Now project onto the screen an image of an animal you know well, perhaps a pet.
3. Study the image until you have a clear impression, then mentally ask his permission to be used as a subject for study. He will usually give hearty approval, but if he should be reluctant, select another animal.
4. Turn the animal around on the screen so you view all sides: first facing you, then toward the right, away from you, toward the left, and back toward the front.
5. Picture a rainbow of color flowing across the screen, from red to violet.
6. Now bring the animal forward until he is close enough to touch.
7. Physically extend your arms and place your hands of light around his head. Study his head, noticing his eyes, his nose, his ears, his fur or hair.

Viewing with X-Ray Vision

1. Imagine that the range of your vision has magically expanded so that you actually have X-Ray vision. You are able to see mentally beyond the surface into the inner layers of form.
2. Focus your inner vision upon the center of your pet's forehead.
3. Now project your consciousness into the bone dimension: imagine, visualize the skull. See it mentally, feel it with your hands. Any way you perceive is correct and effective. You may have the feeling that you are just imagining it, making it up, which is a common reaction. Just flow with your imagining; consider it a game.
4. As you hold the skull between your hands (remember to use your physical hands as well as your mental hands), observe the teeth, the eye sockets, the sutures where the bones of the skull join. Take your time to create a clear impression. Notice the shining white color of the bone.
5. Concentrate your attention again upon the center of the forehead.
6. Now project your awareness into the brain tissue dimension. Visualize, imagine the brain. Place your hands of light around the brain to sense the very special energy emanating from the brain. Recall pictures you have seen which diagram the complex functioning of the brain.
7. Ways of perception vary widely. You may find yourself viewing individual cells, a diagram, or a vivid panorama in full color showing the marvelous complexities of the brain.

If you are predominantly clairsentient, you will probably perceive through your sense of touch, rather than mentally seeing images. Your imagined hands will define an object as explicitly and realistically as if you actually held it in your physical hands.

Whatever your method of perception, it will be consistent

You will continue to perceive in your own unique way whenever you are attuned to the inner dimensions.

8. When you are ready, project your awareness back to the skull dimension, pausing to renew your prior impression, then return to the outer dimension.

Viewing with X-Ray Vision: Torso

1. With your imagination, you can enlarge or reduce the animal to any size which is comfortable for you. He will stay in any position in space in which you place him.
2. Now put your hands around his rib cage, and focus upon the center of the chest.
3. Again project your consciousness into the bone dimension, and be aware of the ribs, the spine, the entire skeletal body. Use your hands to trace the legs, the shoulders, the tail; feel and sense the whole skeletal structure. You will detect any injuries, such as fractures or misalignments, whether recent or healed.
4. When you have made a thorough study of the skeletal structure, focus again upon the center of the chest.
5. Project your awareness to the tissue or organ level, and concentrate upon the heart.
6. Create, imagine, visualize the heart, just as you have seen it in pictures. Place your hands of light around the heart, and attune to the heart beat. You will feel the pulsing rhythm in your hands, giving you a sense of intimacy and closeness to your pet.

   You are viewing the heart as if you had X-Ray vision, observing the awesome wonder of this beautiful, perfectly functioning creation.
7. Now imagine the heart transparent; notice the smooth and delicate operation of the valves, the surge and flow of blood. Take as much time as you wish to behold its wondrous design and perfect harmony.
8. And now for a special experience: imagine the heart gradually increasing in size, larger and larger,

continuing to expand until it is the size of a magnificent cathedral. Observe its grandeur, its exquisite perfection.

9. Now project yourself into that cathedral of the heart. Imagine yourself actually there. What do you feel? Sense the powerful life-force surrounding you, electrifying you with its vitality. You are in touch with the very innermost being of the animal.

10. Spend some time communing with your pet, through this intimate, ultimate communion.

11. When you feel that you have completed the ceremony, project yourself out of the heart, reduce it back to its normal size, and again be the observer, holding the heart in your hands of light.

12. Now focus your attention upon the lungs; hold one lung in each hand of light, and feel the rhythm of the breathing. Perceive the structure of the lungs.

13. Concentrate next upon the liver, placing your hands around the liver and sensing its own individual energy.

14. You may continue your exploration if you wish, especially if you feel that the animal may have a problem in a specific area.

15. You will be able to ascertain the presence of any imbalance or imperfection, and later will learn methods of sending correction.

16. When you feel that you have completed your study, transfer your awareness back to the skeletal level, pause for a moment, then return to the outer level.

17. Project the animal back on to the screen, turn him completely around, and remove him from the screen.

18. Bring yourself out in your usual manner, feeling happy and centered, in tune with life.

* * * * * * * * * * * * * * * * * * *

This is an exciting exercise. It can be almost overwhelming to discover that you are actually breaching the barriers which normally keep us locked into our own separate spheres of perception.

The realization of your accomplishment begins to grow, as you move from your first reaction of incredulous disbelief into conviction that it must be possible, because you are doing it. Reinforce this conviction by repeating the exercise with another animal, and continue to practice with various subjects until you can attune to them without hesitation.

Reactions vary with this exercise. Some people do not perceive as clearly as others, but this is no cause for concern. As they progress with the rest of the exercises, their inner senses will develop, and they will be able to return to this exercise later with more rewarding results.

Remember that each person responds in his own way, and though you are learning to develop all of your inner senses, you will still tend to perceive most vividly in one particular fashion.

How do animals react to this exercise? Is this an invasion of privacy, or are they unconcerned? From our observations, animals seem to know when they have been selected as subjects, for this is a means of communication which they themselves apparently utilize and understand. They usually respond with enthusiasm and show their pleasure in unmistakable ways.

People who work with animals find these skills of inestimable value. They are able to discover underlying causes of illness or injury, and determine the cycles for breeding. They are able to predict the periods of gestation and times of birth.

Veterinarians value these techniques as wonderful supplements to their regular practices. Many veterinarians learn to recognize intuitively the cause of an animal's problem as soon as they see the animal, or even through telephone diagnosis from a distance.

So far we have concentrated primarily upon studying the anatomy of animals, learning first to accomplish this unusual skill. Using the same techniques, you can also communicate mentally with an animal, asking questions, receiving answers, sharing viewpoints and knowledge.

Exercise: Communicating with Animals

1. Enter your meditative level, then project your pet on to your inner screen.
2. When you have a clear impression, turn him around on the screen from left to right, ending with him facing you. See the colors of the rainbow flowing across the screen, from red through orange, to yellow, green, blue and violet.
3. As you study your pet, let your heart expand with affection, and imagine a beam of light flowing from your heart to his. Actually feel the flow of affection strong and clear before you continue.
4. Now bring your pet closer to you, and have him step down from the screen.
5. Now begin to converse mentally with him. He will respond, and you will understand as clearly as if he were actually speaking in words. He will answer questions, will share his problems, his joys and his knowledge.
6. When you have finished your conversation, thank him, say farewell, and return him to the screen.
7. Flood him with the colors of the rainbow, then erase his image from the screen.
8. Bring yourself out in your usual manner, feeling happy and grounded, in tune with life.

* * * * * * * * * * * * * * * * * *

As you practice communicating in this manner, you will one day discover that you no longer need to place your pet upon your inner screen. You will find yourself communicating mentally with him in his actual presence, or whenever you just drop into your meditative level and think of him. When you look into his eyes, you will understand his thoughts, and he will understand yours.

With minimum practice, you will become adept at this technique quickly, opening the door to a wonderful new world. On the inner planes, you have learned the language of animals, and their friendship and wisdom is available to you.

CHAPTER 18
TELEPATHY

Telepathy! What rare and mysterious power enables a few gifted people to communicate with one another through their thoughts? Is this a supernatural, God-given talent, or is this a skill which we may develop and learn?

Ancient teachings tell us that humanity is one great sea of consciousness, and that you and I are each a wave upon that ocean. We are deeply and fundamentally united with one another, yet each shines forth with his own unique, individual radiance, joined and empowered through a common circuit of being.

Because you have been practicing the exercises introduced in the preceding chapters, you have so awakened your intuitive abilities that you may now begin to know and experience that oneness...you are ready to learn and use telepathy.

Telepathic communication takes place upon the same meditative level we have been researching. When you attune yourself to this dynamic level of consciousness, you can be in touch with another person instantly merely by thinking about him.

As you are discovering with so many of the techniques in this book, the methods are simple. You are learning to apply talents you already have...you need only become aware, and use them. Parapsychological research has demonstrated convincingly that highly accurate intuitive capabilities are natural and inherent in all of us.

One classic experiment, frequently conducted in

parapsychology classes, involves two people and requires only that they be able to relax deeply and enter the meditative level.

One experimenter remains in the laboratory, while his partner moves to an undisclosed location. At a preselected time, both enter their meditative levels and think of one another. The sender in the field projects a message, usually an image or impression of his surroundings, while the receiver in the laboratory records his perceptions.

These experiments were done originally to test the abilities of highly skilled psychics, but in the process it was discovered that everyone could do them. Nearly every person who tried was successful, both in sending and receiving.

In this chapter, you will learn how to focus this natural ability, how to project and receive information directly from the union of your mind with the minds of others.

Telepathic Communication Techniques

We will explore two techniques; one method will take advantage of special receptive periods during sleep, while the other more advanced method may be used at any time.

Telepathy Technique #1: Sleep Communication

During sleep, our states of consciousness undulate and change, following a universal pattern which is reflected in our brain waves. As we begin to drift off to sleep, we release our hold upon the beta, or waking state, and plummet directly to the deepest delta level. We remain there for varying periods of time, then move slowly up through theta into alpha.

We stay in alpha for approximately five minutes, then sink softly and gently back through theta into delta. After awhile, the brain quickens and we again move through theta to alpha, then return to delta. This ebb and flow is repeated several times during a normal night's sleep. The time we spend in alpha is gradually extended, culminating finally in one full hour or 45 minutes in alpha, the last hour just before awakening.

This basic sleep rhythm may be used as an avenue for telepathy, for the long period of alpha consciousness is a time of great sensitivity and receptivity to telepathic communication.

Now that you have learned to enter your meditative level at will, you may send and receive mental messages whenever you wish. Your intended recipient, however, may be so engrossed in the outer world that he is unaware of your attempts to reach him. The one time you can be sure of his openness and receptivity is during his last period of alpha sleep before awakening.

Experiment: Telepathy during Sleep

1. Prepare for sleep, then enter your meditative level.
2. Instruct your inner self that you wish to awaken when your subject is well into his final long receptive sleep cycle. Go to sleep in full confidence that you will awaken at the exact right time.
3. If you are still learning to govern your sleeping habits, you may wish to use an alarm clock for added assurance. Set it to a half hour or forty-five minutes before your subject's normal time of arising.
4. Once awake, enter your workshop level.
5. Project on to your inner screen an image of the person you are contacting.
6. When you have a clear impression begin to converse with him mentally.
7. At the conclusion of your conversation, thank him, give him your blessings and let him fade from your screen.
8. Bring yourself back in the usual manner, feeling centered and grounded, refreshed and in harmony with all life.

* *

The messages you send on this level go directly from your mind to your subject's mind, with no interference from the confusion and misunderstanding which occur on the outer level.

Few of us know how to listen, although listening is an ability which can be developed through practice. Professions which demand clear communication, such as counseling and psychology, give their students special instruction in the art of listening, for this invaluable skill is considered essential, a cornerstone of their training.

In normal conversation, the listener's mind moves far more rapidly than the speaker can express his thoughts. The listener hears the words, interprets, evaluates, and accepts òr rejects the information. The words may stimulate a train of thought which will carry him off in another direction. His attention is focused elsewhere, though he seems to be attentive, and the speaker's thoughts make little impression.

Sometimes the listener is so immersed in his own concerns that he hears only part of what is said. Often there is misunderstanding, the perceived message differing totally from that which was intended. Sometimes an emotional response is triggered, disrupting and distorting the communication.

In addition to these obstacles to clear understanding, we all develop protective barriers which filter the information which is constantly bombarding us. Negative past experiences may cause automatic rejection of future communication from these or related sources. Because of an unfortunate encounter with one individual, we may reject categorically whole ethnic groups, occupations, or those with similar physical characteristics. Real communication is difficult and unpredictable through normal channels of conversation.

On the inner planes, however, the channels are open and clear. Messages are transmitted and received in their entirety, with no misinterpretation.

A natural response is to speculate if this might not be a

convenient tool for persuasion, for manipulation and control. Fortunately, nature has provided safeguards so that those functioning on these powerful high vibratory levels can neither manipulate nor be manipulated with these procedures. All of us who are attuned to these frequencies have innate built-in protection, which prevents anything of a negative, destructive nature from reaching us. Only the positive, that which contributes to our total well-being, will be accepted.

Remember, also, that everything we send forth returns to us multiplied and magnified. Thoughts projected from the deeper levels of consciousness carry far greater power than do those emanating from the levels of the rational mind.

If we attempt to use these powers for unlawful manipulation, the adverse reaction will be swift and unmistakable. We will discover first of all that the methods are completely ineffectual, they do not work. Then we will receive the rebound of the negative intentions, which are magnified many times into a truly malevolent force. The resultant disaster is unquestionably of our own making, a direct result of our own misguided efforts. One experience of this nature is usually sufficient to persuade an astute observer that these methods are to be used only for good.

Conversely, rather than attempt to control, others may feel unqualified to use the method altogether due to some uncertainty over the wisdom or appropriateness of their advice. Such concerns need not be a deterrant, for none of us has the omniscience to understand and evaluate all of the issues involved in any situation.

The only qualifications we need to consider are our underlying motives. If we are attempting to help another person, with his welfare as the primary goal, we are motivated by a spirit of caring and compassion. Perhaps our ideas may not be the best resolution of a problem, and thus may not manifest. However, the pureness of intent, the warmth and affection we send forth will be received and absorbed gratefully by the recipient.

The positive energy and power of the beneficent thoughts we project will not only contribute to the solution of the problem, but will return to us intensified. Be free to use the process with confidence and effectiveness.

Most of us direct our first communications to those who are most important to us, those whom we love. Using this process, you have a unique and effective way of expressing that love. You might be hesitant to demonstrate such open affection in your everyday world, but in this world you are totally inconspicuous and private.

So share your true feelings with someone you love, and imagine yourself embracing him as you enumerate the qualities you admire. Then let the sensations of love blossom in your heart, flooding out to enfold and encompass him. Feel the emotion deeply, for this is more than an intellectual exercise.

You are endowing him with the most precious gift you can bestow upon another person, the gift of love. The ramifications of that giving are far-reaching.

Unfortunately, most of us harbor feelings of deep insecurity, an inner conviction that we are not truly loved nor worthy of love. This springs from childhood, as a part of the human condition. Few of us had ideal parents; for all of us (including our parents), though we may be doing our best, are learning and growing. Nearly every parent looks back when his children are grown and wishes he could do it all over. He would rear them quite differently, using the vantage point of life's experiences.

Even those blessed with loving, supportive parents carry insecurities engendered by misunderstanding, rejection, taunts from other children, or scars inflicted from just living their lives. Now we have the means to free one another, to lift the burden of self-doubt and depreciation.

When you send love on the inner planes, the warmth of that love seeks out the hidden recesses of unworthiness and floods them with healing light. As the darkness of self-recrimination dissolves, that person is freed from a prison created by his own lack of self-appreciation. He is now able to love himself.

So take time to lavish this gift upon those who are dear to you. You will notice a remarkable difference when you next see them, for they will radiate a deep inner joy and sense of security which comes from the depth of knowing that one is beloved.

Extend your range beyond your intimate circle, and give healing love to all who enter your world. You have a priceless opportunity to uplift yourself, your friends and humanity as a whole.

Other Uses for Telepathy

You will discover many other uses for telepathy. For example: in teaching children, in helping people overcome undesirable habits, in encouraging those undergoing stress. When using the technique with children, keep in mind that each child is developing at his own pace, according to his own inner tempo. Respect that rhythm, and make no attempt to force him beyond his capacity. Help him, however, with encouragement and praise, to deal with problems and to relinquish outgrown habits. Tailor your approach to the age and personality of the child.

Always speak positively on the inner planes, emphasizing the benefits to be gained from a change, instead of dwelling upon the negative qualities to be left behind.

If a friend is facing a crisis or a stressful situation, reassure him during sleep that he has the strength and resources to master the challenge, that Higher Consciousness is supporting him, and that all will be well.

Children and sensitive adults will probably recall your nocturnal visit and mention it the next day. A child may tell you of a vivid dream, and will repeat word-for-word the message you gave him.

An intuitive adult may realize this is direct communication, and will respond accordingly. He will remember the message when he awakens. Many trained intuitives use this system for regular intercommunication. You will quickly become proficient in conversing with others when they are asleep, and as you observe the gratifying results, the practice will soon become second-nature.

When you have perfected the technique, use it often, for you will be much more efficient, carry far greater impact, and will handle life's issues with notable ease when you recruit the powers of the inner dimension.

Two Methods of Telepathic Communication

We spoke of two systems of telepathy which you will be learning. They can be used interchangeably, but most of us have a tendency to apply them in slightly different ways.

The first system. the sleep communication method, is an excellent way to instruct, resolve problems, and help others overcome habits or handle stress.

The second method is especially valuable for gathering information, for attuning to inspiration and creativity, for ascertaining the true state of affairs and the current concerns of other people. This second system has the advantage of being readily available at any time. Thus you will find it increasingly useful in your daily life.

The first method of telepathic communication takes place on the basic meditative, or alpha level of awareness. In the second method, you will lift your consciousness to the finer frequencies of intuition and creativity, and will contact others on these higher spiritual levels of being.

Exercise #2: Telepathy during Waking Hours

1. Enter your workshop and greet your guides with your welcome ceremony.
2. Sit in your chair, facing the screen, with your guides beside you.

3. Count backwards from 25 to 1, to lift yourself still higher into the creative level.
4. Focus your thoughts upon the person you wish to contact. Soon his image will begin to materialize on your screen.
5. When you have a good, clear impression, when you sense his presence, invite him to descend from the screen and sit beside you.
6. Now begin to converse mentally with him.
7. On this high level of consciousness, only truth will prevail. Your questions will be answered truthfully, information given freely. Since all knowledge is bestowed upon the entire human race, equally available to all, with exclusive rights granted to no one, ask without reservation, and you will receive the answers. Morally and ethically, however, always honor another's privacy, and do not probe for secrets.
8. When you have completed your conversation, thank your guest, put him back upon your screen, bless him, and see his image mist and fade from view.
9. Conduct your concluding ceremony with your guides, then bring yourself back to your outer world, feeling refreshed, centered and grounded, in tune with all life.

* *

This technique is a wonderful way to stay in touch with family and friends and to determine their true states of well-being. Distance is no consideration.

However, you need not limit your communication to people you know. Bring into your workshop anyone of interest to you, the experts and authorities in any field. Contact those who can assist you with your work and hobbies, with exploration and research. Since time does not exist on the inner planes, you may visit with personalities from the past and future as well as with those currently on the earth plane.

If you are involved in the creative arts, use this process as a limitless source of inspiration and guidance. Invite one of the great master artists to critique your work, to inspire you and assist you in perfecting your talents. You might be happily surprised at the results.

A New Renaissance

We are on the threshold of a magnificent New Renaissance, surpassing in wonder anything the world has ever known. As each of us learns to harmonize with the finer incoming energies, we will be able to receive the music of the spheres, the new art, poetry and literature, which will express the grandeur and beauty of our transformed New Age. The influx is already beginning.

Humanity is on the verge of knowing what is beyond mind and body, of learning that we are so much greater than that which we seek. Our developing powers of mind are helping us to understand, to realize that whatever we need will be brought to us.

By attuning yourself to your highest nature, by developing your talents and asking for inspiration, you may help to channel these great treasures to humanity.

Telepathy is more than an exciting, convenient new accomplishment. It is the method of communication of the future. You are developing skills essential for the New Age.

As you sensitize your responses to your fellow human beings through telepathy, you are also serving a higher calling: you are attuning yourself to the Infinite, gaining access to the inherent knowledge of the human race. You are to be in the forefront of this great new emergence.

CHAPTER 19
INNER ANATOMY

With the increasing acuteness of your inner perception, with your practice of telepathy and the projection of your senses into the mineral, plant life and animal kingdoms, you are now ready for the next challenge.

In this chapter you will explore and establish a road map of the human body and mind, discovering as you do your own individual manner of perceiving. Your subject will be a close friend, whose permission you will obtain mentally before projecting him onto your inner screen for study.

You will attune yourself first to the outer dimension, viewing the features, the hair, the general body structure. Then you will extend your awareness to the inner dimensions, and with your clairvoyant X-Ray vision you will study the skeletal, muscular and organic structures, as well as the senses and emotions.

You will be astonished to find the whole body unfolding before you, as you sense its marvelous functioning and learn that you can recognize areas of particular stress or imperfection. You may see literally, in exact detail, or may have your own special symbolic way of perceiving and interpreting.

It is important that you remember to use your hands for sensing as a complement to mental viewing. This gives an added check to those who are primarily clairvoyant; it also develops clairsentience, the ability to feel on the inner planes. Clairsentience seems to accompany the capacity to know, to "have a feeling" that something is so. So use your

177

hands freely, and imagine that you are actually touching the form.

You are ready now to begin. You may ask a friend to read the exercise to you, one who is in harmony with you and the work you are doing. Sit in a quiet, comfortable place, close your eyes and relax for a few moments together. Your friend will begin to read, pausing after each direction to give you time to follow instructions.

Exercise: Studying Human Anatomy

1. Close your eyes, then enter your workshop level with your usual method. Fill and surround yourself with white light from your star. Greet your spiritual guides with your welcome ceremony. Let me know when you are ready to continue.
2. Mentally select a friend whom you know well, and project his image onto your inner screen. Take your time to attune yourself so you see or sense him clearly. Mentally turn him around to the left, away from you, to the right, then facing back toward you.
3. Now mentally ask his permission to be used as a subject. (Permission is nearly always given, but if he should refuse, thank him, remove him from the screen, and select another subject.)
4. Mentally move the subject forward, close to you, close enough to touch.
5. Begin by attuning mentally to the outer body dimension, observing the features, the posture, the general body characteristics of the figure on the screen. Concentrate upon the face, and study the eyes, the nose, the ears, the mouth, the hair.
6. When you feel that you have made a comprehensive study of his face and head, focus your attention upon the center of the forehead. Now mentally project your awareness to the skeletal, or bone dimension, as you

visualize the skull. You will receive a clear impression of the color of bone.

7. Observe the teeth, the sutures where the bones of the skull join, the eye sockets. You will be aware of any problems which need correction, such as dental problems. You will probably be surprised to discover how readily you sense this formerly hidden area.

8. Again concentrate upon the center of the forehead, and mentally project your awareness to the brain dimension. Be aware of brain tissue or cells. Feel the special rhythm and vitality of the brain as you place your hands of light around it. Study the structure, the varying colors, the energy of the brain as you imagine, sense and visualize. Recall pictures you may have seen depicting brain functions. Follow the nerves which connect to the brain. You will have a sensation of actually perceiving the inner operation of this fascinating part of the human body.

9. When you feel that you have completed your study of the brain, project your awareness back to the bone structural dimension, and then to the outer body dimension. Be aware of the facial features, the hair and head.

10. Then extend your arms and imagine that you are placing your hands of light around the rib cage. Concentrate your attention upon the center of the chest. Now project your awareness to the skeletal dimension. See, sense, feel the rib cage, using your hands to sense the ribs. Take your time.

11. Gradually explore the entire skeletal structure, the arms and legs, the spine, the shoulders, the hips. You will be able to determine any imperfections or injuries, such as fractures, arthritis, chemical imbalances, problems with joints or discs.

12. Do not feel hurried. Take all the time you need to do a thorough study. You may feel this is all your

imagination which is a common reaction. Just give your imagination free rein, and know that anything you imagine is fine. There are no set rules or expectations.

13. When you are ready to continue, concentrate again upon the chest, and project your awareness into the lung dimension. See, sense, and feel the lungs. Hold one lung in each hand to feel the rhythm of the breathing. You will sense in your own way any respiratory problems, such as asthma, pneumonia, smoking deposits, or emphysema.

14. Attune next to the heart. As you hold the heart in your hands of light, you will feel the pulse of the heart beat, as well as its vigor. You may imagine the heart as being transparent, and see the functioning of the valves.

15. Enlarge the heart to the size of a room, so you may examine it carefully. You may experience a sense of awe as you visualize and imagine the intricacy and wondrous harmony of the heart. You will notice any imperfections in the heart or heart functions, such as damaged valves, chemical deposits, or inadequacy.

16. Explore the other internal organs in the same manner, the stomach, the pancreas, the liver, the intestines, the kidneys, the gall bladder, the spleen. Use your hands to feel, visualize, sense, imagine. You may enlarge the organs mentally if you wish, to examine more carefully areas of malfunction.

17. Notice the way your attention is drawn to areas of stress or imperfection. You will seem to have a special intuition about these areas. You will not have to seek them out, for they will manifest in varying ways, demanding your attention.

18. When you are ready to complete your trip of exploration, return in the reverse order, pausing momentarily to examine the organs and the skeletal structure.

19. You may check the subject's senses from the outer dimension by imagining that you are looking through his

eyes as if you were looking through a camera. Cover one of the subject's eyes, then check the vision in the uncovered eye. You may examine his hearing in the same manner.

20. If you have discovered any physical problems, this is the time you may send correction and healing. Use any method which seems right for you. You are directing healing energy with your thoughts and imagination. As you imagine the imperfections being corrected, the image will change to one of perfection. Visualize the perfect image strongly, knowing that you have corrected the problem on the etheric plane, and the physical will follow suit. You are sending a very powerful form of healing energy which can do only good.

21. When you feel that you have finished the healing, place your subject back on your inner screen. Turn him around, first toward the left, then away from you, toward the right, then facing. Give him a final blessing, and have him disappear from your screen.

* * * * * * * * * * * * * * * * * * *

You may use this method of mental attunement with any person you know, so practice as often as possible. You will become more accurate and rapid in your assessment as you gain in confidence and expertise. You are creating a framework to be used in your further study of intuitive evaluation and spiritual healing.

CHAPTER 20
REMOTE HEALING

Y ou have now reached the climax of the course. You are learning mastery of yourself and your world, learning to contact higher realms of being. You are treading the path of the adept, attuning yourself to inner sources of knowledge and wisdom, of prudence and discernment.

As you work with the various exercises we have suggested, you are acquiring an imposing array of skills. Each skill opens a door to vast new opportunities which you may expand and develop as you apply them in your life. You are now ready to consolidate these abilities, to use them for communication and healing.

We have spoken of Universal Intelligence, a limitless storehouse of knowledge and inspiration; we speak also of Universal Consciousness, the great unifying sea of Being, of which we are each a part. We have imagined each individual as a wave in this all-inclusive ocean of consciousness which enfolds, joins, and unites us, making us aware that we are all part of one another.

We might also fantasize that each one of us is a light bulb, energized from a central electrical circuit, radiating, shining our light individually, yet all part of one great power. By merely thinking of another person, we are instantly in touch with that person, with no interval of time and space.

You demonstrated this communication through telepathy, and through projecting the image of a friend onto your inner screen to study anatomy from an intuitive perspective. You discovered that you could visualize your friend, mentally speak with him, and extend your awareness into various levels of his being. You have practiced with other friends, and realize that you may contact any of them in this manner.

You are now ready to learn methods for communicating just as clearly with people you have never met, have never seen. You will contact them just by hearing their names, will place them in time and space by knowing their ages and the communities in which they live.

This may seem a miraculous feat, yet you are already interacting constantly with others through your thoughts. Now you will learn to do so consciously and deliberately, and retain full memory of the communication.

You will need a friend to assist you in this exercise. If possible, work with someone who has been studying these methods with you, developing together as though you were students in seminar. You will be tuning closely to one another on the inner planes, so it is important to select a partner who has learned to reach the intuitive level through mystical studies or practice in meditation.

At first glance, beginners may feel that the exercise seems formidable, yet it actually is so easy that every reader is capable of doing it. It is a simple, natural procedure for those who have completed the preceding steps, as you will discover.

Your assistant will have in mind an individual whom he knows, one who has ailments in need of correction. The assistant will guide you, the healer, to your deeper levels of awareness, and will then present the subject to you for assessment. He will tell you only the subject's name, his general address, and his age.

Your assistant will then ask you to attune to the subject, place him on your inner screen, and perceive him with your intuitive senses.

When you have an impression of the subject, the assistant will instruct you to ask the person's permission to be used as a subject. As you mentally converse with the person on the screen, you will probably receive full permission to proceed. Occasionally the request is refused, in which case you bless the subject and let him leave, and your assistant will submit another person.

We have found through experience that we are unable to attune to individuals who withhold permission. Sometimes they will appear on the screen and then slide right off, will peek around the corner from behind the screen, or will shake their heads and state that this is not the right time and that they are leaving. Most subjects, however, are eager to cooperate and are delighted with the opportunity to be subjects.

The assistant then directs you through techniques for scanning the body of the subject so you may determine which areas are in need of correction. You will mention the general areas as you perceive them, then focus upon these selections one at a time, enlarging the section and mentally exploring it to discern the nature of the malfunction.

Each person perceives in his own individual way, and will usually continue to follow his personal pattern of perception whenever he does an assessment for healing.

Some people see clearly, as if they were in an anatomy class, observing the parts of the body as if those parts were actually before them. Some see symbolically, and must interpret what they see. Others do not see at all, but sense or feel, often perceiving through their hands. Some hear voices describing the nature of the illness; while others have an inner sense of just knowing what is wrong. Some see auras or energy fields.

There are many ways of perceiving, each one just as accurate as any other. It is essential that you practice assessment with many different subjects presenting a variety of illnesses, so you can discover and categorize your own responses.

Medically trained readers are often surprised to find that their intuitive perception of anatomy does not coincide with their empirical experience or observation. They may instead see symbolically or graphically; they may perceive through touch or through a sense of knowing.

A busy neurosurgeon, for example, was astonished to find that his perception of the brain with his inner senses differed widely from his way of perceiving with his outer senses. Instead of the neural tissues he was accustomed to seeing in surgery, he saw a great central switchboard, with a complex tangle of wires, switches, and flashing signal lights.

Interpreting what you see or sense is another skill which you may need to develop. The most reliable method of interpretation is to ask your guides the meaning of different impressions. The answers they give will prove to be correct, since your guides are in direct contact with Universal Mind. Even those readers who do not mentally hear their guides speak will receive an answer by "knowing" the answer whenever they ask a question.

As you practice, you will develop your own repertoire of perceptions, cataloging intuitive impressions and correlating them with symptoms.

Feeling Symptoms

Occasionally, individuals who are strongly clairsentient will feel a subject's symptoms duplicated within their own bodies. Some healers may permit such symptoms to manifest within themselves to a certain degree, in the belief that this promotes accuracy in their assessments.

We do not encourage this practice, for nothing is gained from taking negatively charged energy into our own magnetic fields. We intend to remove the symptoms from the subject and then neutralize the discordant energy.

A healer who remains objective and detached, as would a capable doctor or nurse, is able to function much more capably than does one who becomes intimately involved in the problems of the subject. We are compassionate and caring, yet paradoxically resist the temptation to identify too closely with the subject.

Some experienced healers are able to unite with another person, blending and merging with his being, and becoming one with him. This is a valuable and effective technique, but one which is not applicable to our type of healing.

Skilled healers throughout the world who use this method of identifying with a patient are able to absorb the patient's maladies into their own bodies. They then raise their own vibratory rate, and release the illness, freeing the patient from the problem. Such healers often become quite ill themselves in the process. Since we are working with a totally different technique, from another level of being, we keep ourselves separate and free as we concentrate upon eliminating the undesired conditions.

Remember that you are completely in charge of yourself at all times when you function on these levels of mind. You may accept or reject anything you wish, including personal attunement to a subject's symptoms.

So instruct your inner mind that you are the observer only, that your own energy field is completely intact and protected. Remind the inner self that you may attune to a subject through your mind or through your hands, but since your own magnetic field is sealed, imbalanced energy from the subject cannot penetrate this protective shield.

If you find that you are one of the few people who are overly sensitive to symptoms, a simple procedure added to the basic exercise will correct that condition.

Exercise: Strengthening your Protective Shield

1. When preparing to do remote healing, pause for a moment first to visualize yourself enclosed in a bubble of white light.
2. Visualize your hands protruding from the bubble. At the point where your wrists touch the bubble, imagine cuffs which permit your hands to protrude and move freely, but which prevent any exterior energy from entering your bubble.

3. When you have finished your assessment and healing, rub your hands briskly together to remove the vibrations of the subject.
4. Flick the excess energy into the ground, then bring your hands back into the bubble.
5. You have separated your energy fields, retaining only the positive glow of the compassion and healing energy which has flowed through you.

* * * * * * * * * * * * * * * * * * * *

In addition to this special precautionary measure, the basic exercise itself contains another safeguard which is so effective that few need additional supplementation. It will remove any remaining residue one might possibly retain. The last step in your healing ceremony is to step into a crystalline shower of brilliant white light, which will cleanse, align, and vitalize your whole being.

Sending Healing

With the assessment completed, you are ready for the most important part of the exercise, sending correction to the areas of malfunction you perceived. You may use any method you wish. Your inner consciousness will direct healing energy in the proper amount to the area you designate, using any symbol or process you imagine. Many techniques will work. For example:
Some people like to work with light or color. Others prefer intricate instruments and machines of their own invention. Some people work with ointments and drugs, while others replace defective organs with new organs from a bank in their workshops.
You may dissolve kidney stones or gallstones and flush them away, erase dark spots, sweep calcium deposits from joints, and blow tobacco smoke from lungs. Allow free range to your imagination, applying your remedies until you

perceive the area restored and functioning normally. See the image perfect in all ways. You are actually in touch with the subject's etheric body, the blueprint which is the model for the physical body. When you correct imperfections in the etheric form, these corrections will manifest in the physical form.

As you visualize the ideal image, you will be pouring the quality of perfect beingness into his being, creating that perfection. Your gratitude, plus your knowledge that in reality it has been done, will reinforce the power of the correcting process.

One of the most exciting steps in the ceremony is your request to the subject on the screen that he tell you the underlying reason for the problem. This is the great stumbling block in all types of health care.

We may diagnose and treat the symptoms, but a patient is not cured until we have uncovered the deep basic reason for his trouble. An illness may be healed, only to recur or manifest in a new form, often repeatedly. Health practitioners go to great lengths attempting to learn the fundamental causes of problems, but these causes often remain obscure.

You, however, can discover the underlying reasons easily, directly; all you need do is ask the subject on the inner plane. . . . and he will tell you.

Often the true effectiveness and power of your healing projections will be demonstrated vividly and unmistakably. On these occasions, your subject will show unexpected and dramatic improvement at the exact moment you are sending healing. All those involved are thrilled by such an event, but for you, the healer, it offers the final, uncontroversial proof you may have needed, proof that the system really works.

You will have such experiences. You may well be overwhelmed when you discover that the healing you have been sending is not just part of an intriguing game. . . . it is powerful and real.

So now you are ready to begin, to discover the joy and

excitement of one of the most rewarding adventures you
have ever experienced.

Directions for Assessment and Healing

1. Find a quiet, peaceful place, where you will be
   undisturbed. Sit facing your friend, your assistant.
2. The assistant mentally (without speaking) chooses a
   person he knows who has ailments in need of healing.
   For the first few episodes, it is best to select subjects
   whose principal problems are physical; later you can
   work with those who have emotional and mental
   difficulties.
3. He will read to you the instructions in the exercise. Each
   time you do the exercise the same directions will be used,
   for during the time the inner mind is learning this
   process, it will respond most readily to repetition of the
   same format.

Exercise: Intuitive Assessment and Healing

The assistant will read the following directions, pausing
after each direction to give the healer time to respond:

Directions

1. Close your eyes and enter your sanctuary-workshop by
   your usual method. Greet your spiritual guides with
   your welcome ceremony.
2. Imagine over your head your radiant, 5-pointed star,
   one point pointed upward. See it glowing, pulsing with
   light. Feel your body filled with light, the great bubble of
   light around you, with beams radiating from you. You are
   a center, a channel for light. Take your time and tell me
   when you are ready. (Both will enter the meditative
   level. When healer has completed his greeting
   ceremony, he will tell the assistant that he is ready to

proceed. Assistant will open his eyes and continue).

3. I will now count from 1 to 12 to help you relax and ascend to a high, peaceful level. With each number, visualize yourself ascending steps. 1 - 2 - 3 - 4 - 5 - 6 - 7 - 8 - 9 - 10 - 11 - 12.

4. You have now reached your deep meditative level. You will be completely successful in attuning to the person I will be presenting to you as a subject, and will be correct and accurate in your intuitive assessment and spiritual healing.

5. When I count to 3, the subject will appear on your screen.
   The name of the subject is: _____
   The age of the subject is: _____
   The community in which the subject lives is: _____
   The subject is (male or female): _____

6. 1 - 2 - 3.
   The subject (name):   _____
   Age: _____
   Address (community) :   _____
   Sex (male or female):   _____
   is now on your screen.

7. Use all of your senses as you visualize, imagine, feel, create, sense the image of the subject on your screen. You are able to see it clearly. Describe to me what you see.

8. Ask his permission to be used as a subject. (Subject usually agrees; if he should refuse, Assistant will direct healer to thank the subject, remove him from the screen, and then give another subject.)

9. Turn the subject completely around on the screen. Flood the screen with a rainbow of color.

10. Now move your eyes rapidly up and down, once a second, as you mentally scan the body of the subject, from his head to his toes, and back to his head. Continue scanning while you develop a clear impression of the subject.

11. While scanning, mentally ask yourself, "On which section of the body does my attention seem to focus?"
12. Mention any area which draw your attention.
13. Now focus your attention on one of those areas, and enlarge that area. Notice anything in the expanded area which seems to attract your attention.
14. Describe to me anything you see or feel. Keep talking as you explore, for talking will help you to be accurate.
15. You may feel that you are just imagining, making it all up. This is fine. Tell me anything you are sending. Keep talking, and use your hands.
16. When you have studied one area which attracts your attention, move to another area and study that area. Enlarge it, and tell me all of your feelings and impressions.
    (Assistant: when assessment is accurate, answer, "That is exactly right," or "You are correct." If inaccurate, respond: "All right," "Okay," or "That could be correct; I do not have all of that information at the moment. Tell me more." Never respond with "Wrong," "No,", or "That is incorrect." Always be positive and supportive.)
17. Now scan the image starting at the head. Check each area of the body, noticing any areas of imperfection or imbalance.
18. Enlarge any area you wish to study more closely, and describe to me whatever you see or sense.
19. Ask your guides to interpret anything which is unclear. They are there to help you.
    (Assistant: if symptoms do not seem to fit subject, have the healer check his mental calendar. To attune more closely, repeat today's date and the subject's name and address.)
20. When you feel that you have completed the investigation, you are ready to send correction and healing to any areas of imperfection, malfunction, or imbalance you may have noticed. Sense any

malfunctioning part of the body returning to perfect function. Use your imagination to send correction and healing in any way which seems right to you. Let your final impression be one of health and perfection.

21. Visualize the perfect image strongly, knowing that you have corrected the problem on the inner plane, and the physical will follow suit. You are sending a powerful form of healing energy which can do only good.

22. Ask the subject the underlying reasons for his problems.

23. (Assistant: evaluate the information perceived, pointing out correct assessment, noting again the healer's method of perceiving those areas of imperfection discerned. Mention other areas you know to be in need of correction.)

24. When you are ready, give your subject a blessing, then remove him from the screen.

25. Whenever you clear your screen of a subject, you separate your energy fields, and you are both clear and free. You each retain the positive glow of the healing energy, the compassion, and the blessings which have been channeling through you.

26. Your guides now place you in a cleansing shower of brilliant white light, showering you with blessings and correcting any imperfections or imbalances you may have.

27. Whenever you do this exercise, you receive personal benefits on many levels of being. You are projecting compassion, loving concern, and an intensely powerful wave of healing spiritual energy to another person. This positive energy returns to you multiplied many times, as a beneficent influence in your life.

28. You will become more accurate and rapid in your assessment and healing as you gain in confidence and experience. Your inner growth on all levels will be accelerated as you give care and healing in this manner.

29. Thank your spiritual guides, have your closing ceremony, receiving their blessings, and bring yourself

out in your usual manner. You are happy, alert, revitalized, in perfect health; you are centered and balanced, in tune with all life.

* * * * * * * * * * * * * * * * * * * *

As you open your eyes, you will probably experience a wonderful feeling of exhilaration and vitality. You have just accomplished a major feat, in spite of your possible doubts or indecisions. You have proven to yourself that the things you have studied are possible, for you yourself have actually put them into effect. You no longer believe and hope; now you know.

If you have been working with a friend who has been studying with you, trade roles so that you are the assistant and he the healer. Then present a subject to him for intuitive assessment and spiritual healing. You learn and grow through performing each role.

Do not stop with your first encounter. Each of you should work with at least three subjects before you conclude your beginning session. You are consolidating all that you have learned, and need a minimum of three transactions before you feel securely proficient.

Your energy has peaked, so accomplish as much as you can while you are finely focused. Your abilities will increase at a surprisingly rapid rate. Arrange your schedule so you will be able to repeat the session as soon as possible.

When you have worked with ten subjects, you will have progressed far beyond your skill at two or three, and will have reached a plateau of ability. You will feel much more secure in your competence.

When you have worked with twenty subjects, you will feel that you are almost professional, and will proceed with confidence. When you have worked with thirty subjects, you will have crystallized all of the skills you have been developing, and from that time forth you will be adept in the art.

When we reflect upon the rare and remarkable accomplishment you are perfecting, this seems an amazingly brief time in which to master this skill. Your results will depend not upon calendar time, but upon the frequency and number of assessments you perform.

As you apply these techniques, you are working with powerful natural laws of the inner dimensions. Improvement and learning usually develop gradually when we practice a skill, but you are working with a special force when you send love and healing to another person. As that generous outpouring floods back to you multiplied and magnified manyfold, your health will improve and your abilities increase at a truly astonishing rate. If you were merely practicing exercises for your own growth, you would progress at a normal pace, but you are rewarded beyond measure when you give of yourself to another person.

As you acquire expertise as a channel for healing, you will experience other changes which you may not have foreseen. These changes are subtle, and you may not be aware of them until your friends begin to notice and comment.

Expect to experience personality changes, to find your attitudes and values undergoing alterations as those issues which once were paramount lose their attraction, and are replaced by others of a completely different nature. You will attain harmony and balance, a sense of purpose and deep contentment which you have not known before. You will see the world through new eyes.

In a most unusual and enlightened manner you are fulfilling the divine dictum to "Heal the sick", and in so doing are bringing radical transformation into your own life.

CHAPTER 21
CONCLUSION,
BUT JUST BEGINNING

You have now finished the book and completed a course of instruction which will increase immeasurably in value as you apply its principles, thereby bringing magic and splendor into your world. You are perfecting new skills, developing new talents, discovering your powers to create.

Apply the methods you are learning to all aspects of your life. These remarkable techniques can bring harmony to the intricacies of daily living, can strengthen and guide you through your most demanding challenges and crises. By means of these same processes you will also be able to serve your highest goals, to find your deepest knowing.

Soon the skills embodied in these exercises will become second nature to you, readily available whenever you wish, with no need of ceremony or preparation. At that time, the structured procedures which were so helpful for you in the beginning will seem cumbersome and superfluous. As your reliance upon processes diminishes, you will gradually modify and then discard these aids. The lessons they have taught you are now an intrinsic part of your very being.

After a time, you may notice an unexpected cyclic rhythm in your pattern of spiritual development. As you move into a new stage of growth you might find that you gradually lose your expertise in skills you had acquired in previous stages. This is a common occurrence and should be no cause for alarm. Nature is simply freeing you from distraction and compelling you to focus your attention upon your current phase of development. Talents once gained are never lost, however, so whenever you actually need them, those skills you perfected in the past will be instantly available. Your life will become increasingly richer and finer as you broaden the horizons of your personal world. You are taking the High Road, a springboard which lifts you above the slower, more ponderous evolution of the majority of human beings, as they struggle to free themselves from the encumbrances of a lesser age in preparation for the glories of the incoming age.

You have entered the accelerated pathway trod by pioneering spirits, the enlightened souls who are actively bringing into manifestation our new order of being. You have joined them on this privileged pathway, on the cutting edge of creativity. With your rapidly developing abilities, your every thought and action can aid in the design and creation of our glorious new world.

When you began this study, you may have been motivated by various reasons, ranging from faint curiosity to burning zeal. However, once you tasted the joys of self-discovery, you probably found yourself committed to the most engrossing pursuit of your entire life. In your search for inner knowledge, you have touched the deepest yearning of the human heart, the longing to awaken to the essence of your own Pure Being.

With each step you take, you are awarded further glimpses of the glory and magnificence residing within the sanctuary of your own divine nature. Each step reveals another of the great mysteries, for you encompass within yourself the grand design of all creation. The mystics have truly said that as you learn to know and master yourself, you uncover and master the secrets of the entire universe.

You are engaged in the most important undertaking of your life, preparing for a quantum leap in consciousness, the rebirth into a new dimension of being, an experience far beyond anything you can envision. You are involved in the culminating dream of mankind's entire saga upon earth, the goal which has been sought and longed for, for centuries. You are deeply blessed in your pilgrimage, for you have available to you spiritual assistance and guidance unprecedented in the history of humankind.

Your personal progress is reflecting in miniature the royal journey, the progressive development of all humanity. We are advancing inexorably from the primitive stages of being, through the discovery and gradual unfoldment of our inner resources and powers, to the final awakening and at-one-ment with our Higher Selves.

Yet rewarding as each phase of your personal unfoldment may seem to you, its full impact is even more far-reaching than you probably realize. For as you develop and awaken to higher states of consciousness, each step you take causes a ripple of reaction throughout the entire human race. You are so deeply interlinked with the whole fabric of humanity, that as you transform yourself, you help to transform the entire world. Each discovery you make instantly reverberates throughout all of us.

The study of holograms is revealing wondrous new insights which substantiate the ancient teachings proclaiming that we are in truth one body, one unit of being. The role each of us plays is unique and vital, essential to the well-being of the whole.

The people you meet, the lives you touch, are affected by you presence in more ways than you can imagine. Your influence extends far beyond the furthermost reaches of your vision. You are altering the course of the world's development forever by your Being.

By consciously endeavoring to uplift your own consciousness, you are doing more to bring peace to the world, to assist humanity into the bright realization of our incoming Golden Age than any other venture you could possibly undertake.

What we have shared is just the beginning . . . you

yourself determine the ends. You have laid a solid foundation, acquired the basic attributes you need for this tremendous adventure.

May you travel in blessing, living in the light, on this most absorbing journey of all time. May you reap its wondrous bounties as you follow your destiny's path to its supreme culmination, the ultimate rapturous reunion with your own True Self.

SEMINAR INFORMATION

After reading the book, you may wish to attend an Illuminated Mind Seminar.

Under the guidance of a trained teacher and in the enhanced energy of a group of participants, your progress in mastering the techniques will be greatly accelerated.

For further information and Schedule of Seminars in your area, please write:

Illuminated Mind Seminars,
8462 Larch Avenue,
Cotati, CA 94928.
Tel: (707) 795-0357

If you would like to have details sent to a member of your family, or a friend, please give the name and address below:

Name: _____
Address: _____
_____